A BETTER KIND OF VIOLENCE

THE CHICAGO SCHOOL OF POLITICAL
ECONOMY, PUBLIC CHOICE
AND THE QUEST FOR AN ULTIMATE
THEORY OF POWER

FILIP PALDA

Published by *Cooper-Wolfling*. None of the advisory board of *Cooper-Wolfling* are responsible for the opinions expressed in this text, which remain the responsibility of the author.

Editor: Kristian Palda
Typesetting and final design supervisor: Filip Palda
Proofreader: Kristian Palda
Cover design and typesetting: Filip Palda. Set in Minion Pro.

About the cover: The cover is Apollo, a complex Greek deity representing both the quest for knowledge and the controlled use of violence.

Palda, Filip, 1962–
A Better Kind of Violence / Filip Palda.
Includes bibliographical references.
ISBN 978-0-9877880-7-8

WWW.COOPWOLF.COM

About the author

Filip Palda earned his Ph.D. in economics at the University of Chicago.

Dedication

TO MY WIFE MARIA, WHO HAS GIVEN ALL OF HERSELF WITH LOVE
IN MY FIGHT

CONTENTS

About the author iii

Dedication iv

1 WHY 1

2 LEVERS OF POWER 6

3 PIGOU VS. COASE 26

4 REGULATION 46

5 TOTAL MODEL 70

6 PUBLIC CHOICE 100

WHY   1

T HE RATIONALE FOR WRITING this book is to summarize
for the first time the efforts of the two major schools of
thought in economics vying to devise a complete theory
of political power and to mention a third that is waiting on
the sidelines. One is called Chicago political economy and the
other is called public choice. The third is called mechanism
design. This is not a survey of the whole of any of these fields
but rather an overview of what unites them and the central
principle that divides them, namely that governments evolve
towards the efficient application of force, or, a better kind of
violence.

The origins of the book go back to early 1981, when my father
was a visiting professor at Virginia Tech. He invited me for
my February undergraduate break at Queen's University in
Kingston to have a look at a new type of scholarship develop-
ing called public choice.

I was 18, a second year economics student and intrigued by
anything that smacked of the application of economics to politics. I attended a seminar in a wood panelled house at which
Murray Weidenbaum, then Ronald Reagan's economic advi-
sor, delivered a funny but serious lecture about the seemingly
boring topic of regulation and the interests that guide it. To
this day the memory brings to mind Lord Kenneth Clarke's
observation that in the Gothic period serious issues could be
approached with a sense of play.

Present were two figures of authority who after the talk introduced themselves to me as James Buchanan and Gordon Tullock. Their questions seemed so erudite and exotic that I knew this was a field I wanted to learn more about. It held the promise of understanding government by using economic tools. I then based my undergraduate thesis on a public choice topic and I published it in the journal *Public Choice* under Tullock's guidance. Three years later I found myself starting my Ph.D. at the University of Chicago. Gary Becker had just published his 1983 article on interest groups and the struggle for power. It was the capping achievement in a field that would become known as Chicago political economy and which though similar to public choice would enter into conflict with it. Five years later I completed my doctoral dissertation with Becker by becoming the first to apply his model to campaign spending issues. Before leaving I told Becker that his article had provided me with what I saw as a complete theory of power and that I was astounded by its prediction that governments will tend towards efficiency. He shook his head in disapproval and lamented that this is not what his article said and that no one really understood it. It might have helped then if he had not written that "Political policies that raise efficiency are more likely to be adopted than policies that lower efficiency."

I thought about Becker's *cri de cœur* on and off over the years that followed. Finally I returned to his article to see what he might have meant. What I found in re-reading it was a degree of nuance that allowed him to say that policy tends towards efficiency while at the same time identifying forces that can thwart it. Was this a profound piece of work or an overly complicated way of formulating the thought that in politics anything can happen? To help me and my students understand the issues better I wrote a short guide to Becker's paper. In writing it I realized that Becker's article, though simply written, was exceedingly difficult to grasp. It seemed to spring directly from the author's head. Context was missing. To really understand it someone would have to first realize that Becker was building on the works of several economists before him. He was coming at the tail end of a debate with its genesis in the 1920's. It would also help to know that Becker's ideas were not universally accepted. They were considered pathological by prominent scholars in the public choice field, most notably Charles Rowley, former editor of *Public Choice*.

Thus I conceived the idea of the present book. Becker's article would not be at the center of the book but would be shown to be one in a sequence of works that has come to define what is now called the school of Chicago political economy. Because Chicago political economy and public choice use the same analytical tools and evolved in lockstep, public choice would assume a prominent role in this book.

What is fascinating about Chicago political economy, and what merits attention is its unrelenting application of economics to politics and the realization of how many results and insights can be squeezed out of such a minimalistic theory. Economics is based on the existence of constraints within which individuals seek to maximize their well-being. The result of this striving is known as equilibrium. With these three principles (maximization, constraints, equilibrium) Chicago political economy is able to build a theory of power. This theory can be used to ask whether competition in election campaigns should be limited, whether increasingly efficient policies will encourage excessive government growth (the Leviathan debate), and it allows us to identify which groups in society are most likely to be preyed upon by other groups. It also allows us to compare the effect of different constitutions on the efficiency and size of government. It warns us not to judge the efficiency of a public policy by textbook economics but rather to compare the waste of a seemingly inefficient policy against the alternatives (a minimum wage may be the best way of redistributing money if the system of taxation is inefficient). At the heart of the theory is the prediction that government policies which are efficient have a good chance of displacing inefficient policies.

Though the idea of politics tending to efficiency is the central idea of the book I do not allow it to overwhelm and ultimately bore the reader. Instead I want to tell a story of how an obscure academic spat over the question of whether governments should intervene to correct "market failures" led to the creation of the economic analysis of private institutions. Ultimately this field was transposed to the study of government institutions where, ironically, the conclusions of free-market thinkers about the efficiency of government converged with the views of interventionist thinkers from the school of cost-benefit analysis.

I also want to show readers how the related field of public choice reacted with growing horror to what it viewed as a misapplication of market economics to politics. Particularly revolting to public choice scholars is the Chicago view that the efficiency of political markets means that policy advice is irrelevant.

I explore this claim in more detail than has been done in the literature to date. While I do not survey all of public choice I show readers what the field is about and focus my description of public choice on one of its central tenets, namely that governments will tend to grow like Leviathan and that the only way to combat this growth is induce inefficiency (yes I mean "inefficiency") at the constitutional level.

I could of course have made this book a sequential exposé of the ideas of Chicago political economy and public choice, but I find survey works to be tedious to any but non-specialists. I prefer to tell a story of the evolution and interaction of both schools of thought, with primary attention on Chicago political economy because it has always caught public choice scholars off guard and forced them into a reactive posture. I believe that the differences between the two schools are exaggerated and I show how closely they mesh. The analysis in my book is wholly original in the sense that no one has bothered to put Chicago political economy in its proper intellectual context and to emphasize its efficiency predictions as being among the most important ever made in the social sciences. I end the book with a look towards the future which may belong to a third field known as mechanism design.

The above is a logical summary of the book but is perhaps not the last word on it. The economic search for a theory of power has electrified my thoughts for decades and I want to share some of that live current with readers. The book will present the reader with habits of thought that allow one to understand not just politics, but history, law (I will be relying on William McNeill's prescient work *Plagues and Peoples* to demonstrate this latter point). Just as importantly, the book is an adventure through intellectual history. It is the first to trace a line from Pigou to Chicago political economy while paying due attention to the parallel but branching field of public choice.

LEVERS OF POWER   2

THIS BOOK IS ABOUT AN attempt to fuse economics and politics into a single theory of power. Karl Marx thought he had achieved this synthesis, as did thousands of intellectuals who devoted their lives to tidying his thoughts. The field was left to them for most of the 20th century. They seemed to be doing well until economists started looking into the matter.

Economists are uniquely suited to creating a theory of power because of two great advantages they have over competing social sciences such as politics and sociology. The first advantage is mathematics. All terms must be defined and all relations between terms laid bare in equations. The grip of this logic admits no sloppy argumentation. Economics does not use mathematics for its own sake but rather to impose discipline on a train of thought.

Writings in political science and sociology may be entertaining but they can quickly loose coherence because they lack a mathematical basis. A grand intellectual enterprise such as fusing economics and politics to create a total theory of power needs the help of mathematics to make sure thoughts remain consistent.

The second advantage economists enjoy is a mastery of what one might call social accounting. Societies are groups of people bound to each other for some positive reason. Humans calculate whether they are getting more by staying in society than they are putting into it. If the balance is negative for too many people, a society crumbles.

Economists inadvertently discovered how to calculate these social balance sheets when they developed the analysis of demand and supply. If you are going to develop a theory of power, you need to know the calculations people are making because everything is connected. If the economic balance sheets tilt in their minds so will the cohesion of different bands of people competing for dominance in society. Economics and group action, also known as politics, are inseparable.

But how do you unite supply and demand, and politics even if you have all the economic tools at hand? The answer has come at the end of a road travelled for fifty years with no clear destination in sight. No economist sat at her desk, sharpened a pencil and scribbled out an ultimate theory of power in a bout of inspiration. Almost no great idea in any science springs like Athena from the head of her father.

The rocky journey to an ultimate theory of power began in the 1920's when Cambridge economist Arthur Pigou tried to break away from free market economics. The task took discipline because Pigou was of two minds. He was a master of free market thinking. He understood the ability of private markets to balance a multitude of needs and means without waste. Such "market efficiency" however could be impeded if the ledgers of social accounting started to get out of balance. An efficient exchange in a market was one in which at least one person was left better off and no one else was left worse off. The fancy term for this was Pareto efficiency. But sometimes exchanges produced collateral damage. If I buy paper from a pulp company that pollutes water, someone downstream who is not a party to our exchange will suffer material damage. The market exchange looks efficient, but when you factor in the costs of pollution social ledgers may tip into the negative. Pigou thought the problem lay in prices that misled buyers and sellers into socially harmful exchanges. A corrective tax to increase the price of paper would sensitize consumers to the costs they impose on others and they would cut back their consumption.

Whether he intended to or not, Pigou outlined a theory of how government and the economy should interact and hinted of some unification between economics and politics. Yet, therein lay the conceptual limitation of the exercise. Government was seen as an impartial, all knowing, benevolent force intervening to benignly correct market imperfections. His followers began to write of a "central planner" who used demand and supply analysis to correct "market failures".

Few at the time noticed it, but these first attempts at fusing economics and politics were going astray. They confused what government "should" do with what government "would" do.

This distinction was noticed by Ronald Coase of the University of Chicago. He believed that there was little need for direct government intervention in the economy provided that courts protected property. He saw incorrect market pricing not as a failure of markets but as a failure of government to protect the interests of property owners. Pollution would not be a problem if its victims could claim adequate compensation for damage to their property. Property rights were not a cure all. It is expensive for government to define and defend property. But Coase warned that the problems of leaguing to government the power to levy corrective taxes and provide services to the public could be greater than those attributable to market failure.

Exactly how much worse would government be as a guardian of the economy than would an imperfect private market?

Coase did not answer that question. It was left to his successors at the University of Chicago to pose it. What they found seemed a contradiction of everything Chicago free market thinking stood for: "Political policies that raise efficiency are more likely to be adopted than policies that lower efficiency." Gary Becker wrote those words in 1983 in an article that would crown Chicago's quest to produce a theory of power melding economics and politics.

Nothing could have seemed further from the verbal whippings Milton Friedman was laying on governments in his contemporaneous book and television extravaganza for US public broadcasting entitled *Free to Choose*. Despite Friedman's evangelical dislike of government, he had a scientific side open to what appeared to be Becker's shocking repudiation of Chicago's free market thinking. That was perhaps because he saw in Becker's statement the inexorable, even ironic endpoint of Chicago reasoning. If Pareto-efficiency was a driving force in private markets, why should it not be so in politics? Chicago thinking was catholic. That which moved a merchant could move a bureaucrat. Becker, building on the work of his colleagues George Stigler and Sam Peltzman showed how the worlds of politics and commerce could be reconciled and melded.

Few noticed Becker's article at first, but as with most of his writings it eventually sent shock waves through the social sciences. While the public may have heard of rock-star economists Thomas Picketty, author of *Capital*, and Steven Levitt, co-author of *Freakanomics*, few outside academia know Becker. Inside academia he is a legend. Milton Friedman said that "Gary Becker is the greatest social scientist who has lived and worked in the last half century." High praise coming from someone who was niggardly with it. Friedman taught many future Nobel Prize winners and in some cases made it clear he was less than impressed with them as students. But in the case of Becker, Friedman could write that he "has a brilliant, analytical mind; great originality ... and a profound understanding of both the operation of a price system and its importance as a protection of individual liberty."

The quote is embarrassing in its superlatives. Yet Friedman was no lickspittle. Becker dazzled him. The source of Becker's ability to impress others was not simply the power of his intellect. There is an armada of clever economists whose names are forgotten. Does anyone remember Lester Thurow, shooting-star economist of the 1980's who wrote *The Zero-Sum Society*? Becker's power lay in his relentless application of the three principles of Chicago reasoning. In his 1982 survey of Chicago thinking Melvin Reder called these "tight prior". Chicago believed that individuals maximized their well-being, that they did so subject to material constraints, and that the mass interaction of individuals led to an equilibrium in which no one was willing to change his allocation of resources given the allocations chosen by everyone else. These were the anchors of Chicago thinking and almost no amount of contrary evidence could unmoor those who had chained themselves to these principles of markets.

The logic behind Becker's and the Chicago school's analysis of politics was that crime and politics are intimately related. In both fields there are human predators and prey. But there is a twist. Predators gain less than the prey suffer. A lobby group that manages to get a million dollars from government benefits by a million dollars. But the businesses that pay this tax lose a million and may also go bankrupt and lose the work of a lifetime. This asymmetry in gains and losses from predation gives victims a built-in advantage. Victims will hire rival predators to protect them in exchange for a fee, much as did poor villagers in Kurosawa's movie *The Seven Samurai*. So a "market" in protection services will arise in which predators who inflict less collateral damage will out-compete their more virulent rivals. Becker saw in such a process the emergence of increasingly efficient political systems. But the efficiency was tainted. It arose not from mutually benefiting exchanges, as occur in the private market, but from competition between bullies for domination of their victims.

It is important to use the qualifier "may" when claiming that Chicago political economy predicts increasing efficiency. The basis of this claim is that victims have a built-in advantage. They suffer more than predators gain. But if that were the only force in play, victims would crush their oppressors. Predators need to be endowed with some special advantage of their own. One such advantage is that small groups with concentrated interests in gaining government favor are more easily mobilized than the large groups they prey upon. A few thousand molasses farmers gain tens of thousands of dollars from US government laws that restrict the importation of foreign sugar, whereas millions of consumers suffer a price increase costing each of them perhaps no more than a few dozen dollars.

The asymmetry in per-capita benefits from political action gives certain interest groups a stronger "power function", that is a raw ability to influence government with given resources than others with a weaker power function. In Chicago political economy, a political "equilibrium" is reached when some sort of balance is struck between the advantage victims feel due to the asymmetry of gains and the advantage that predatory groups enjoy due to stronger power functions. The level of government efficiency that results depends on the importance of both these forces in the final equilibrium. Put differently, government does not attain the greatest level of efficiency possible in the use of resources, but rather the greatest efficiency possible for the power functions that are in play. This could mean that a great deal of efficiency is achieved, or if the power functions are very strong, that efficiency is very low. So, the Chicago view has in mind a wide spread of possible efficiency outcomes.

Why Chicago political economy is important

CHANGES IN EFFICIENCY in the Chicago model arise when either of several things happen. The power functions of predators and victims change, or the economy changes in such a manner that the inbuilt advantage of victims increases. That is when the real action starts.

You could call these changes "political revolutions" that shift the balance of power between groups. A clear example is the fall of Bronze Age nobilities who had monopolized the few sources of tin and copper needed to make edge-taking weapons from the resulting alloy. The monopoly was lost when metallurgists discovered how to mine and smelt iron, which is one of the most abundant minerals. Inexpensive swords and armor flooded the weapons' market. With their enhanced power, large groups with iron weapons challenged bronze-based nobilities in wars that lasted centuries. Much damage resulted from the conflict. Ultimately leaders who taxed more efficiently, and at reduced rates, came to dominate. Thus, shifts in the power function led to both harm and increases in efficiency. The theory does not specify which is larger.

Yet to speak of political revolutions as the sole motor driving change in government efficiency is to ignore the manner in which the economy is tightly wound into the balance of power.

It is possible that the collateral damage from predation will rise as an economy develops. Economic development happens when new, cheaper ways of doing old expensive things are discovered. The fall of trucking and air regulation in the US during the 1970's can be attributed in part to innovations in transportation. Cheaper ways of providing these services were being discovered but regulation restricted who could enter the market, thereby profiting existing producers and workers' unions. Despite their highly developed political power functions they lost their bid to keep out competitors. The gains being suppressed by regulation, that is, their collateral damage, became so large that victims were galvanized into action. A similar pressure for change was felt by Soviet Bloc countries. By the late 1980's citizens of these countries became aware of the growing rift in wealth between themselves and the West. Even though the authorities had the guns, "people power", the intrinsic advantage of victims, prevailed. The more general principle at work in the cases of regulation and the Soviet bloc is that stifled economic development can lead to productive political upheaval.

Coase and the structure of power

STUDYING POWER FUNCTIONS and collateral damage can give researchers an idea of how politics and economics evolve towards the good as these functions change. The study of both sides of political equilibrium can also help us understand how political institutions evolve and how this evolution influences power and efficiency. This is the most difficult strand of Chicago thinking to understand. It is rooted in the work of Ronald Coase. He believed economists were too fixated on abstractions such as supply and demand. He suggested that to understand how free markets allocate resources through voluntary consensus we need to study the institutions that make them run. The institutions we see have evolved to minimize the "transaction cost" of doing business. He argued that firms exist because they limit contracting costs. Workers in a firm cooperate on a voluntary basis with each other. No contracts need to be drawn up between them for the millions of cooperative acts needed to make a company run.

Chicago thinking took Coase to the next level by using his analysis of market institutions to ask what sort of political institution minimizes the costs of determining the allocation of resources through the coercive decision mechanism of government. Referenda and citizens' initiatives are democratic institutions that allow large groups of voters with diffuse interests to counter the concentrated interests of small, heavily vested groups. Devolving government power to the lowest administrative level is also an institutional change that evens the playing field between large and small groups. By limiting political predation and the collateral damage it entails, the evolution of democratic institutions such as decentralization and direct democracy could be seen by Chicago scholars as a quest for greater efficiency in government.

The dragon's den

ANY BRANCH OF economics claiming to explain the evolution of government and the structure of political institutions would seem to be of vital importance to policymakers. If you know the ingredients of good government, then a society can build its own and enjoy the benefits. In fact, this is the approach taken by current pop-historians and global visionaries such as Francis Fukuyama. In his book *Political Order and Political*

Decay he produces a shopping list of five conditions for a modern, functioning "nation state" to master the intricacies of power. All of this comes after several hundred pages of examples from which he distills the essentials of state influence. He is an exponent of a tradition of list makers stretching back to Edward Gibbon's 18th century oeuvre *Fall of the Roman Empire*.

If a nation follows Fukuyama's to-do list will it benefit from the exercise? Chicago political economists says "no". Their reasoning derives from the efficient markets hypothesis which says that stock prices immediately integrate all information relevant to company performance. This means there is no useful information in prices that will allow you to predict future prices. If there were, then someone would already have used that information and the result would be then reflected in the price.

When applied to government this reasoning leads to the conclusion that there are no "big bills left lying on the sidewalk", to use the phrase coined by Mancur Olson. Even if you see a nation rich in natural resources, where the people are impoverished, there is nothing you can do to advise them on how to improve their condition. If such an improvement had been possible it would already have been implemented. US advisors in Afghanistan learned this lesson the hard way. Despite being endowed with over twenty trillion dollars' worth of mineral resources and receiving close to a hundred billion dollars of US aid, Afghanistan's resources might as well be on the moon. Its political equilibrium includes groups with power functions that overwhelm the intrinsic advantage of victims. What appears like wealth for the taking is more like gold in a dragon's den. Though those outside the den may be dressed in rags, they are living as efficiently as they can, given the constraint imposed by the dragon.

Public choice

SOME PEOPLE DO not fully agree with Chicago political economy. They belong to a field called public choice. They apply economic reasoning to political phenomena. In most ways, they are like scholars from Chicago political economy. What chafes public choice scholars is the claim that politics has a compass pointing towards efficiency. Even more odious in their view is the nihilistic conclusion that policy advice is irrelevant. To Charles Rowley, former editor of the journal *Public Choice*, Chicago's "… interpretation of the political process emanates from a fundamentally flawed application of … microeconomics to the political marketplace … while the *Journal of Political Economy* publishes papers that defend the U.S. federal farm program as an efficient mechanism for transferring income to poor farmers, there is justifiable cause to worry whether CPE [Chicago political economy] scholars and their journal editors ever look out from their ivory towers and survey the real world."

To Chicago political economists there is no mystery about why big bills are lying on the sidewalk but somehow society cannot pick them up. Chicago sees these unattainable bills as simply a result of the existing reality of power relations. There is no point in fretting over their presence. Being unobtainable they are not in fact lying on the pavement.

Public choice scholars take a more pro-active view. They believe that big bills on the sidewalk result from poorly conceived "rules of the political game" such as constitutions, and from what they see as the great awkwardness of satisfying individual needs through group decision processes. Those who should be proposing rules and limiting government incursions into private affairs are none other than public choice scholars.

In this way, public choice researchers embed themselves into their own research agenda. They are active participants in the political phenomena they study.

While Chicago remains agnostic, public choice scholars yearn for a creed to solve the world's problems. To James Buchanan, the prominent exponent of public choice, the creed of public choice is to restrict "Leviathan". According to Hobbes, Leviathan was an oceanic creature that grew without bound. To public choice it is a metaphor for a government that seeks to maximize its revenues with little concern for the wellbeing of its subjects. Along with Jeremy Brennan, Buchanan argued that politics is a "two-stage" game. In the first stage rules should be written that restrain the ability of governments to tax as they please. Such "tax constitutions" might tie the hands of politicians in the second stage of the political game. Without the ability to follow the advice of economists for creating taxes that are efficient, in the sense of minimizing disruption to economic activity, the Brennan-Buchanan restriction might appear retrograde. However the benefits of these restrictions is that they avert an even greater damage to society. There is no guarantee that in the second stage of the political game politicians will follow the advice of economic technocrats. They may instead become part of struggles between interest groups trying to bend the tax system to their own advantage. The efforts expended are known as "rent-seeking". Such rent-seeking costs may far exceed the efficiency gains from leaving politicians free to possibly create an efficient tax system.

Brennan and Buchanan championed an inefficient tax system stitched into the DNA of the constitution because they had little hope that politics would ever strive for efficiency. Political "markets" are riddled with intractable inefficiencies due to the need to mobilize large numbers of people to make collective decisions. The cost of being informed about policy is high and the benefits to voting are low. In even the most democratic countries, pathologies abound which make it impossible for collective decision making to efficiently satisfy the needs of citizens.

The one hope that Brennan and Buchanan held onto was for a people to create a built-it system of harm-reduction right at the start of a political system. It was an idealistic stance of the sort which is absent from Chicago political economy.

Mechanism design

WHILE JOUSTS WITH public choice take place within the shared analytical framework of classical economics, there lurks a faction plotting not only to subvert but to overthrow everything that Chicago political economy and public choice stand for. Its influence is still not widely felt, but it poses a challenge. It is called mechanism design. It is conflict politics in the style of Machiavelli. Personal, cynical, and full of wiles and strategies.

Its application to politics arose out of the works of political scientists at the University of Rochester in the 1960's but its deeper origin lies in a branch of mathematics called game theory. Economics explores how individuals maximize their wellbeing subject to the constraint of personal budgets. It is impersonal in that people have no control over their environment. Prices and incomes are determined by equilibrium conditions arising from monolithic relations between masses of people. Individual choice takes place in a setting where mass relations are determined by impersonal institutional arrangements which cannot be tampered with or influenced. First year economics students know these institutional arrangements as supply and demand equations.

Game theory is about how individuals dispute a prize in a struggle where the constraint is the intellect of the opponent. Such a constraint is malleable. What I think can influence what the other thinks which influences what I think and so on. Game theorists discovered that this sort of interaction between people may produce a solution to the game called Nash equilibrium. It is a state in which no one wants to change his or her strategy given what they anticipate the strategies of others will be. Some games produce Nash equilibria which truly represent the best use of resources. Strangely some equilibria are perversely inferior. All participants realize that a different outcome could benefit all contestants but no one seems able to negotiate the path to this better outcome. Game theorists extend these thoughts to politics and conclude that the pathologies of power struggles can be palliated by the application of something called mechanism design. Some also call this reverse game theory. It is about bribing or fining people to abandon conflicts and align their interests with each other---also known as the search for "incentive compatibility".

Mechanism design sounds like the public choice and Chicago notions that higher order rules should be found that minimize the collateral damage from lower level struggles for influence. But there is a fundamental difference. By basing its analysis on the behavior of masses both public choice and Chicago political economy can be tested. There is ample information on mass behavior and a certain regularity to it. Mechanism design isolates itself from empirical verification by relying on what are basically highly mathematized stories of irreproducible one-on-one interactions. It is a manifestation of the Platonist notion that some very smart people can devise rules to herd people into behaving in the herd's own interests. It is one of several new creeds of government interventionism

but rises above all others by its ability to tell a story. It is daz-
zlingly creative and possessed of an impeccable logic. Its basics
need to be grasped to see how Chicago's incomplete treatment
of inferior Nash equilibria can be rounded out.

A roadmap to this book

AT THE START of this chapter I wrote the vague phrase that this
book is about an attempt to fuse the sciences of economics and
politics into a unified theory of mass behavior. Several pages
later the objective remains unchanged but the path to take is
clear. This book will focus on Chicago political economy.

Recently its importance has been recognized in citation
indexes. According to Kim and colleagues the three foundational articles of Chicago political economy were written by
George Stigler, Samuel Peltzman, and Gary Becker. These articles rank respectively 14th, 27th, and 44th among the most
cited in economics over 1970-2005. Despite these impressive
numbers we are far from knowing who the winner is in the
contest for the best theory of power.

The public choice of Brennan and Buchanan is a powerful
contender and mechanism design bides its time on the sidelines. Yet like a star athlete who commands attention from
opponents everywhere on the field, drawing them to him,
Chicago political economy must be the focus of this vitally
important clash of ideas. Behind its seeming nihilism one senses a probing method of thought that heightens our senses and
enables us to spot hidden truths. The basis of the method is to
keep in mind that the skilled redistributor of resources keeps
collateral damage to a minimum. Thus, Chicago thinking goes,
if power goes to those who wield it efficiently, history can be
deciphered as the march towards the measured use of violence

in society. Great states rise on their abilities to extract monies from their subjects in a minimally intrusive manner. Taxes, constitutions, criminal law and civil law, monies for the poor, bridges and roads may seem like great enterprises in the public good. In fact, they are devices for capturing and redistributing wealth. The public good plays a subservient but supporting role in the rise of the modern state, which itself is the result of a competition among predatory groups.

Chicago thinking also allows us to probe what appear to be mass pathologies lasting for generations. A dictator who gasses innocent villagers and represses democracy may be a monster. But would a civil war be preferable in which a hundredfold more might perish? Chicago political economy exhorts us to look beyond these shocking pictures of groups in turmoil.

The stability we see, however tainted with brutality, may result from alliances built over centuries and a kind of customary application of state violence that has been dialed down to the lowest level consistent with peace. We may then focus on the central question which Chicago political economy leads us to. Namely, what is the root cause blocking a group of people, a society, from engaging in fruitful cooperation?

The plan of the book is as follows. At the heart of Chicago political economy is the interplay between politics and economic efficiency. Chapter 3 explains what economic efficiency means; how markets may fail to attain efficiency; Arthur Pigou's views on how government can restore efficiency to the economy; Ronald Coase's objection to Pigou; how Coase forced economists to think about how institutions such as private firms evolve to minimize the transactions costs involved in attaining economic efficiency and how his analysis of efficiency in private markets opened the door to a new generation of scholars who applied his ideas to government efficiency.

In chapter 4 the focus is on George Stigler's *The Theory of Economic Regulation*, which contained the basic assumptions and logic of Chicago political economy. The most difficult and contentious assumption is that all of government activity is simply redistribution of money. Considerable effort is devoted to explaining the thought behind this assumption. The chapter also introduces the notion of a political equilibrium as being the balance between power functions and the inbuilt advantages of victims. This chapter is a springboard to the first mathematically unified statement of Chicago political economy, which is Becker's *A Theory of Competition Among Pressure Groups for Political Influence*.

Chapter 5 is devoted largely to explaining Becker's article but is not a slavish reproduction of it. The key concept in this chapter is the meaning of political equilibrium. It arises from a game-theoretic interaction between clashing interest groups and has very specific implications for the efficiency of government. And it depends critically on a seemingly obscure "second order condition" which is the increasing harm imposed on victims from equal accruing increases in taxation. This largely neglected feature is what makes Becker's model work. I will not hide from you that despite being a masterpiece of simplicity Becker's model is difficult to even begin to understand. Conveying its essence clearly is the challenge of this chapter.

Chapter 6 is devoted to public choice. It is not a survey of the entire field. Rather it summarizes the public choice view about the difficulty of achieving efficiency in politics. This is enough to give the reader a taste of public choice while allowing us to remain focused on the central theme of this book, namely Chicago political economy's conception of political equilibrium. This chapter suggests that public choice is not in contradiction with Chicago political economy but rather is a subset of possible political worlds admissible under the Chicago political economy approach to power. The chapter also presents a detailed discussion of Brennan and Buchanan's competing Leviathan model of politics. This will necessarily entail a brief detour into the classical theory of optimal taxation which was developed by public finance economists who had no concept of how their theories would be used in the field of public choice.

Particular attention is paid to the public choice notion that thinkers such as themselves can make a difference to public policy. Keynes believed the same. He wrote "Practical men who believe themselves to be quite exempt from any intellectual influence, are usually the slaves of some defunct economist. Madmen in authority, who hear voices in the air, are distilling their frenzy from some academic scribbler of a few years back". Is there any evidence to support this public choice view apart from personal testimonials? The answer to the question goes straight to the heart of the question of efficiency in politics and the meaning of statistical tests of efficiency. Chapter 6 concludes with a brief discussion of mechanism design and how it contrasts with Chicago political economy and public choice.

Further reading

Becker, Gary S. (1983). "A Theory of Competition Among Pressure Groups for Political Influence." *The Quarterly Journal of Economics*. 98:371-400

Brennan, Geoffrey and James M. Buchanan (1977). "Towards a Tax Constitution for Leviathan." *Journal of Public Economics*. 8:255-273.

Coase, Ronald H. (1960). "The Problem of Social Cost." *Journal of Law and Economics*. 3: 1–44.

E. Han Kim, Adair Morse, and Luigi Zingales (2006). "What Has Mattered to Economics Since 1970." *Journal of Economic Perspectives*. 20:189–202.

Olson, Mancur (1996). "Big Bills Left on the Sidewalk: Why Some Nations are Rich, and Others Poor." *The Journal of Economic Perspectives*. 10:3-24.

Peltzman, Sam (1976). "Toward a More General Theory of Regulation." *Journal of Law and Economics*. 19:211-240.

Pigou, Arthur C. *The Economics of Welfare*. First edition 1920. Fourth Edition 1932. Palgrave MacMillan. 2013 Kindle Reprint.

Reder, Melvin W. (1982). "Chicago Economics: Permanence and Change." *Journal of Economic Literature*. 20:1-38.

Rowley, Charles K. "Public Choice and Constitutional Political Economy". Pages 3-31 in *The Encyclopedia of Public Choice*. Edited by Charles Rowley und Friedrich Schneider. Springer. 2004.

Stigler, George G. (1971). "The Theory of Economic Regulation." *The Bell Journal of Economics and Management Science*. 2:3-21.

PIGOU VS. COASE   3

THE PURPOSE OF THIS CHAPTER is to trace the origins of Chicago political economy back to an unlikely source. The reader will learn it is the unexpected by-product of a tussle in 1960 over some obscure points in markets economics.

The antagonists in the tussle were the then living Ronald Coase and the shadow of Arthur Pigou who had just passed away. Coase was little known in economics. Pigou had some fame among economists from having written *The Economics of Welfare* in 1920. The book is a masterpiece of applied supply and demand analysis. Pigou's mastery of this idiom imbued in him a highly developed respect for the abilities of markets to tally the costs and benefits that real world people must consider when making hard economic decisions in mass situations and also alerted him to conditions in which demand and supply represented faulty social accounting due to something called "market failure". His work radiates through economics in a more natural and penetrating manner than that of most of his contemporaries, including his young admirer Keynes. Perhaps this is why Pigou's book provoked attack in 1960 from that other master of economic intuition, Ronald Coase, of the University of Chicago.

Coase was not troubled by Keynes. But in Pigou he sensed a threat that few other market advocates seemed to perceive. He feared that once its arguments became widely understood, and accepted, *The Economics of Welfare* would give governments a free pass to intervene in markets. Its author had to be taken down a peg; no matter that he had passed away the year before. Coase did not know it at the time, but his spat with a spirit over markets would lead to the creation of a theory of political power and a Nobel Prize.

In this chapter we follow Coase as he hounds Pigou. To do this we must gain an understanding of the "social accounting" Pigou devised in order to correct what he saw as failures of the free market. These corrections led to a form of economic efficiency named after Vilfredo Pareto, an earlier economist who discovered the concept.

Coase agreed that markets fail but pointed out that this did not mean governments could succeed any better at correcting these failures. Markets failed when people failed to reach deals that reflected the true costs of the items being transacted. These deals often failed to go through or generated harm because something called a "transaction cost" interposed itself between some parties affected by the deal. If a developer sold to a house buyer but the septic tank installed leaked into a river, riparian rights might be violated but too costly to enforce. So what looked like a deal that created wealth could in fact destroy wealth by devastating a downstream commercial fishery. Coase believed that "institutions" such as courts, and private methods of resolving disputes would evolve to reduce transactions costs and allow the benefits of market exchanges to be realized. Coase argued that governments had no special advantage in resolving such property rights issues because they might face equal or higher transactions costs than did the private market, costs such as the cost of organizing the political consensus to take action.

Though Coase was primarily interested in private markets, his thoughts extended naturally to understanding why certain forms of government, such as democracy and dictatorship, exist. Governments are institutions for allocating resources removed by force from the population. Given the demographic and sociological circumstances of a country, different forms of government might have an advantage over other forms in minimizing the costs that rival interest groups faced when transacting between themselves how public spoils should be divided. In this chapter the reader will become steeped in Coasian thinking so as to be prepared for its application in later chapters to the creation of an ultimate theory of government power. We now rejoin Coase in this examination of Pigou.

A mild case of interventionism?

WHAT WAS THE nefarious work by Pigou that troubled Coase and subsequent admirers of capitalism? *The Economics of Welfare,* when read carefully, turns out to be a meek plea to create a system of correctives for some of the uglier aspects of free markets. Pollution, monopoly, cheating, lying were all forms of "market failure".

Pigou reasoned that markets in their perfect condition are supposed to ensure that if two people make a trade then both benefit and no one who is not party to the deal is harmed. Correct prices were the means by which people coordinated their behavior in a mutually fruitful manner. An economy where exchanges benefitted all would build a growing positive ledger of wealth. If while creating wealth for some, private exchanges imposed collateral damage upon others on a persistent basis then impoverishment and collapse would follow behind. For in such a society people could not use prices to coordinate their actions fruitfully. My purchase of a polluting product was not based on the harm its production did to others. Thus my unmoderated consumption reflects a lack of coordination with those who are suffering. Pigou proposed a system of corrective taxes and subsidies that would sensitize market actors to the effects of their decisions upon other people. This system would entice everyone to act as if they took into account the economic fallout of their decisions, thus creating a complete and balanced system of social accounts.

While not rejecting Pigou's logic, Coase felt that Pigou was looking for solutions in the wrong place. Instead of seeking the help of some benevolent government that would step in to correct skewed prices, the market could take care of the problem if people were able to receive compensation for damages to their property. The Pigou solution tried to impose correct prices from the top-down. Coase believed these prices might emerge from the bottom-up. Whether they did or not depended on the "transactions costs" people faced in reaching deals with each other to avoid needless waste. People would devise institutions and mechanisms such as courts, property rights, social customs to minimize these transactions costs. Instead of looking to some abstract entity such as "government" which provided "correct" market prices seemingly at zero-cost, Coase advocated a realistic assessment of the cost of devising institutions, be these private or public, that minimized the costs people faced in reaching mutually beneficial solutions to conflicts regarding resources.

The Coase-Pigou debate was important because it catapulted economics into its next stage of development. Out of an abstract discussion of social accounts arising from supply and demand would emerge a practical appreciation of how institutions, whose existence had been taken for granted, such as government, the law, private companies, and markets, emerged from the quest to keep to a minimum the costs of transacting all forms of exchange between people. This next phase in economics led to revolutions in game theory, culminating in something called mechanism design. It inspired Nobelists Elinor Ostrom and Walter Williamson in their separate quests to understand why institutions arise. How do you design institutions to minimize the costs of organizing cooperation between large numbers of people? But more importantly, the transaction cost approach to institutions was the basis upon which Chicago political economy would develop its claim that governments evolve towards providing policies that are economically efficient.

What is economic efficiency?

BEFORE WE CAN fully understand the contribution of the Coase-Pigou conflict to the creation of a total theory of power, we need to see what all the fuss was about.

It was about Pareto-efficiency. Given the right circumstances institutions might evolve to foster this sort of efficiency. But what is it and is it desirable? We need to make a detour into this topic. It is essential for the comprehension of all that follows.

The concept of economic efficiency can be stated in a line or two, but skimming over the idea will not allow us to master the elements of Chicago's view of how power determines the allocation of resources. We need to take a leaf from the expository techniques of E.T. Bell, who wrote *Men of Mathematics*, and Paul de Kruif who wrote *Microbe Hunters*. These and other masters of scientific exposition believed that theories could not be dissected as one would a cadaver in an anatomy lesson of Dr. Tulp. The need for these theories must be made plain and the painful steps in their evolution must be traced to arrive at a mature and sympathetic understanding of what they are about. To understand economic efficiency, which is at the heart of Chicago political economy we must ask why economics was created. The answer depends on the appearance of a need for such a science two hundred years ago.

Some might feel an apology is in order for subjecting the reader to such a discursion. None is needed. Economists are poor expositors of the foundational concept of their science. A few minutes spent learning what economic efficiency means, and its broader significance, is time well, and enjoyably spent. What you read below may surprise you.

The creation of economics

ECONOMICS WAS BORN in the British industrial revolution of the late 18th century. There had been no need for such a science before. What might seem like a lack of curiosity by thinkers before then was really just a lack of urgency and necessity. The world changed little. Relations between people in Britain had been stable. The sons of blacksmiths became blacksmiths. The poor bred more poor and the rich entailed their wealth to sons who were expected to repeat the process. For the most part people of different classes retained their memberships therein and entered into stable long-term relations with other classes. Markets as we know them now barely existed. There were occasional farmer's markets, an organized wool and corn trade, construction guilds in some cities. But there were no regular commercial upheavals that put in question the social order. Without perceptible challenges to that order there was no demand for a science that would be of help in managing dangerous economic changes. People of the time could not even have conceived of what such a science would look like. Economics would have made no sense.

The degree to which a market economy was present in any period of history before the 19th century is somewhat of a speculative exercise which nonetheless is the fruit of many decades of work. In *The Livelihood of Man*, an early foray into this subject, Karl Polanyi argued that despite certain archeological evidence such as Hammurabi's legal code, there is almost no evidence for developed markets in pre-Roman antiquity.

Modern research has been led by Peter Temin. In a 2006 survey of Rome and other historical economies, he argues that while there were some product markets in medieval Europe, factor markets, that is markets for labor, were very rudimentary. The use of labor was largely dictated by feudal lords or determined at the village level by the challenges of communal projects in which an egalitarian contribution of effort was expected of everyone in draining fields, building storage structures, and defending against intruders.

According to historian Norman Cantor, even product markets had a limited audience. They were dominated by the demands of about three hundred super-rich families who contracted with millions of artisans, and labourers for delivery of made to order products. The limited degree of market development in medieval Europe meant that relations between the lord-purchaser and the lower-class producer solidified with time and created a significant barrier to the entry of new competitors. Such relations tended to solidify and fit in with the overall static nature of pre-industrial society.

When the industrial revolution got rolling social confusion about change called for some thought. Innovation created wealth but put sluggish firms out of business. The unemployed uprooted themselves from their native communities to find work. A disgruntled urban proletariat formed. Activists began questioning the fairness of the new economy. Politicians asked whether it were not better to restrain commerce. A demand arose for explanations.

Social accounting

THE ATHENIANS HAD been down this path to discovery during their great period of commercial rise. They erred by attempts to explain change in terms that were more personal than social. The works of Sophocles and Euripides are profound examinations of individuals who feel trapped in their new social roles.

In Britain and Europe some analysis more oriented towards mass reorganization was called for. The intellectual community of the day rose to the challenge by sketching the outlines of what might be called social accounting. The analysis of masses was helped along by the development of the science of statistics. It was reaching maturity during the 19th century, partially under the impetus of insurance companies seeking to lower costs through the use of actuarial tables.

Social accounting sounds grand but is really quite simple. Societies are groups of people bound to each other by a mixture of self-interest , which can be broadly defined to include altruism if one thinks about that carefully, and compulsion. Each person keeps a ledger of what he or she puts into society and what he or she gets out of it. People may not be happy with the balance in the ledger but as long as some critical number of them believe the status quo gives them more than the alternatives, a society will persist.

When the social accounts fall too far out of balance the ties that bind people to each other dissolve. Revolution or civil war may ensue. A new set of social ledgers and method of social accounting will have to be devised in order for society to form again.

History can be seen as the search for functional systems of social accounting adapted to different settings. To date there seem to be three types of accounting that cover most situations. Karl Polanyi called them reciprocity, redistribution, exchange. Reciprocity is usually enacted within the system of the village, or the tribe. You scratch my back, I scratch yours. No money is needed because accounts can be kept in the mind and enforced by the simple expedient of expelling anyone who violates them. Redistribution is a form of social accounting generally realized through an institutional structure known as central planning. Exchange generally takes place in a free market with private property under the rule of law. Describing Polanyi's work, Temin explains that "Reciprocity is an informal system in which people aim toward a rough balance between the goods and services they give and receive, with relative values determined by social obligations and traditions that change only slowly. Redistribution is a system in which goods are collected by a central authority and distributed by virtue of custom, law or *ad hoc* decision. Exchange is the set of economic transactions in which people voluntarily exchange goods and services either in barter or for money." Each system presents its members with different rules for calculating the advantages and costs of cooperating with others. Each system lasts only so long as a critical number of people calculate that the advantage of working in society exceeds the costs of staying in it.

Pareto's big idea

PRIVATE PROPERTY UNDER rule of law produces a form of social accounting that has a very specific quality. No exchange of property happens unless it profits at least one person and harms no one else. Such exchanges are said to be "Pareto-improving".

Once all mutually profitable exchanges have been exhausted, society attains an equilibrium which is "Pareto-efficient". This is another way of saying that social accounts are in balance in such a manner that there is no room left for mutually enhancing increases in wealth.

To see how this efficient balance comes about, economists worked out the elements of supply and demand analysis. When a valued product is scarce, consumers are willing to pay more for it than it costs to make. Producers and consumers can split the difference. Such a difference is the sign that further mutually benefitting exchanges are possible. Producers continue to increase their output until what consumers are willing to pay for the last unit produced falls to just slightly above the cost of production. But before the price settles to that "equilibrium" level at which no further consumption or production takes place, money continues to change hands so long as consumers feel they are paying less than the maximum they are willing to pay. Producers are making profits because they are selling at prices above their minimum acceptable level (i.e. their costs). All these trades take place by mutual agreement and harm no one. At the equilibrium price all trades have been exhausted. No redistribution of resources can take place to benefit one person without harming at least one other person. The lack of further opportunities for mutual gain is what makes equilibrium efficient in the sense of Pareto.

Supply and demand analysis induces somnolence in undergraduates. Their interest would spark if professors boasted. The discovery of the Pareto-efficient property of market equilibrium is the first rigorous statement in the history of thought about the forces that keep a society together. For all his bombast, Marx could never put a slide-rule to his soliloquies about social injustice. Measuring their social preoccupations also defied French physiocrats, British mercantilists, Machiavelli, Cicero, and Plato. They wrote with erudition but only words came out, not numbers. Market equilibrium analysis puts social accounting on a mathematical footing. Economics professors would ignite a bonfire of interest if they further explained that social accounts exist to coordinate behavior between people. Whether we speak of reciprocity, redistribution, or exchange, people orient their efforts towards activities that show a positive balance in the ledger. Thus the state of a ledger that concerns many people becomes a guide to mass, coordinated action.

Pigou has a thought

THE NEW TALK of economic efficiency made possible by Pareto, and the maturing concepts of demand and supply allowed Pigou to launch his attack on the efficiency of markets.

Efficiency relied on everyone feeling the costs of their actions. Profit and loss motivated and chastened market actors. That was the only way to preserve resources and guide them to where they were most valued. A market failure blinded the entrepreneur to the true cost of her actions. Pigou said that government could correct that lack of insight through a tax. Supply equations showed the cost to producers of making their product and how they would react when prices changed. Pigou showed that these selfish reaction functions could be repurposed to reflect a social need. All you had to do was to "hack" into the private supply (cost) curve a corrective tax reflecting the monetary damage wrought by a market failure such as pollution. The supply curve then shifted and a new optimum could be calculated. Based on this blackboard reasoning, governments could impose an "optimal tax" that would guide the market back to an efficient state. Put differently, if government could identify where market prices had gone awry, then in supply and demand curves it had an advance warning system pointing to situations where coordination between masses of people seeking wealth might unravel. "Optimal" taxes and subsidies would point people once again in a direction of balanced social accounting that respected Pareto efficiency.

The above sounds somewhat technical, but nothing less than the soul of economics was at stake. Pigou was quietly laying claim to the golden formula for guiding society to prosperity. The eccentric don was putting himself in the front rank of social philosophers. Mathematics of the optimal society was nothing to be sneered at. Even Plato had not given that a shot.

Enter Coase

COASE THOUGHT THAT Pigou was prescribing a false remedy for an imaginary illness. The famous "Coase theorem" states that no matter who owns a property subject to pollution, the final level of pollution will be optimal in the sense that neither polluter nor polluted could benefit from any change in the level of offensive emission. If a train casts sparks that burn a farmer's crops, should the government fine the firm so that it is made aware of the imbalance in social accounts it may create? Coase said not at all. If property rights are such that the farmers are entitled to compensation from burnt crops the railway will continue to run engines that burn crops, provided the profit from these runs exceed the compensation required to farmers. This situation is Pareto efficient because no one is hurt in this scenario and at least one party gains. If railways own the right to cast sparks will they burn crops wantonly? Not at all was the answer. Farmers will be willing to pay the railways to reduce runs so long as the value of burnt crops is larger than the loss from reduced traffic. This was another Pareto efficient scenario. Even if there is no government to impose a fine or corrective tax, the farmer who resists sparks mindlessly forgoes potential payments by the railway. Economists call these lost revenues opportunity costs.

Here then is the crux of the Coase argument. Opportunity costs make themselves felt no matter who owns the land provided property rights are clear. Even without any government to uphold property rights the incentive remains for those who devastate some property to restrain themselves in reaction to payments offered by those who suffer.

To many economists then and even now it has never been clear what the big fuss over the Coase theorem is. Markets tend towards efficiency. So what? This is a valid question. The answers remain tentative to this day. The first is that the theorem alerted economist to the concept of a "Coasian bargain". Roughly what this means is that some sort of mechanism such as a market with well-defined laws about property, can be used to smooth the way to negotiations between parties disputing some resource. The Coasian agenda is one of identifying institutions, such as property rights, that will smooth the way towards agreements. In the jargon of the literature, institutions influence the transactions costs associated with disagreements over the use of property. In early history when the institution of property was ill defined, stable agreements were difficult and a great deal of fighting and nastiness causing needless harm was associated with disagreements over property. In the Coasian perspective, institutions evolved to minimize the costs associated with resolving such disputes.

Another reason for the importance of Coase was that he provided practical validation for something known as the second welfare theorem of economics. This theorem had been proved ten years before Coase by Kenneth Arrow and Lionel McKenzie. Their version was a highly abstract proof showing that no matter how property rights are assigned, a Pareto optimum will eventually be reached. More formally, any Pareto-efficient allocation of resources can be "supported" by a competitive equilibrium.

What economists took home from this was that economies based on markets were like self-sealing tires. Every time some shock came to upset claims to ownership, such as might happen in war or times of rapid innovations that put in question who is the rightful inventor of some great new product, eventually people will exchange their property rights or negotiate new rights in a manner that attains Pareto-efficiency. The insight was of great importance to economists of post-Soviet countries making the transition from state to private ownership. They learned that a redistribution of ownership shares in the economy would initially be inefficient but would tend towards an efficient outcome through Coasian deals between owners of these shares.

Perhaps Coase's greatest contribution was the habit of thought he inculcated by tracing the path from property rights to efficiency. He heightened the economist's awareness of what might today be called the "ecology" of markets. Under the smooth curves of supply and demand lay institutional crags. The principles of the social calculus of mass coordination lay in supply and demand, but the details of how those principles were enacted depended on the means available for people to meet, agree, enforce contracts, and disseminate information between them on where the best deals were to be had.

This ecology could be so complex that any attempts at government intervention to correct a perceived "market imperfection" had to be thoroughly worked out to be justified. If a Coasian saw a smokestack she had to muffle her cry for government to intervene with some tax on emissions or an anti-pollution regulation. Perhaps the costs to government of figuring out the correct tax were costlier than if private interests were allowed to work out some deal with each other to mitigate the "negative externality" from pollution.

To Coase the academic knee that jerked at every seeming market failure needed a brace. One had to be sensitive to market inefficiencies of course, but one also had to be sensitive to the imaginative abilities and creative possibilities of solutions to externalities arrived at by private negotiation and consent. There was no doubt that private markets might get the calculations wrong. But so might governments. When neither could manage you might get a complete breakdown of civil order.

Organizing large numbers of people to cooperate with each other is a costly and complicated business. Sometimes the "coordination costs" are so large that chaos ensues. Coase wanted people to think about what sorts of institutions would at very least avoid chaos, and at best minimize the costs people face when trying to negotiate some use of resources that appears to be in everyone's interest. Was voluntary cooperation or coercion the answer?

Coasians and government

IN ASKING HOW transactions costs molded private institutional structure Coase advanced to but did not cross the fringes of the study of government institutions. His main concern had been with private firms. Supply and demand remained in the picture, though somewhat in the background. They represented the forces of cost and desire that drove people to exchange resources with each other. Coasian analysis sought out the most efficient framework in which these exchanges could take place. In fact, it was narrow and sterile in Coase's view to talk of supply and demand without imagining the buildings, contracts, laws, infrastructures, and social customs in which voluntary exchanges played out and social accounts found their balance.

But what of the involuntary exchanges of resources, if this phrase even makes any sense? Did Coase's method apply? The question had to be asked because a good case can be made that people do not get to use all their resources as they please. Rather, some, or perhaps even all, resource allocation takes place under the ultimate threat of force. British historian John Keegan gives this view elegant expression in *The Mask of Command* where he writes "But, remote though the battlefield is from the marketplace and the court of law, its pre-existence, or the potentiality of recourse to it, underlie all assumptions citizens make about the order of things as they find them. Force ... provides the ultimate constraint by which all settled societies protect themselves against the enemies of order, within and without (pages 311-312)".

Clearly the use of force removes us from the world of mutual understanding where Pareto-efficient, voluntary exchanges are the norm. Perhaps though, the deviation is not quite as extreme as we might imagine. After centuries of conflict with Mongols raiding their borders the Chinese empire gradually settled on a mix of bribes to Mongol leaders and threats of violence by Chinese armies that had raised their level of military competence. These bribes can be seen as "Coasian deals" that protected Chinese rice paddies while enhancing the revenues of Mongols. These deals were not possible in the initial phases of conflict between the two peoples because Chinese and

Mongols had no clear way to communicate with each other. Diplomatic channels were "noisy" and problematic. In economic terms the "transaction costs" of doing business were prohibitive. The result was needless destruction of Chinese property by Mongol raiders in search of wealth, and a consequent reduction in booty available to the horse warriors. The orderly transfer of taxed income from China to Mongol lands evolved through lengthy trial and error as did the institutions for reducing the transactions costs of coming to mutual agreement. But once these patterns were established they proved remarkably stable and both people managed to exchange ideas for improving each other's conditions.

A multiplicity of examples can be found to push the controversial message that even in politics there is an impetus for institutions to evolve in order to minimize needless conflictual entanglements between determined opponents in conflict over resources. It emerged that when Coase's analysis of private markets was applied to governments, the outlines of a remarkable "post-Coase" theorem emerged. There were forces prodding governments to seek interventions that tended towards Pareto-efficiency, the hallmark of what markets strove to achieve. History did not follow doctrines imagined from an armchair by Marx or by fist-pumping idealists manning the barricades in 1848 and 1968. It followed the dollar. That was the fundamental force pushing governments towards Pareto efficiency. Political scientist and historians did not want to hear this. Economists by and large lacked the culture to even begin to grasp the issue at stake. Yet there it was. Economics put politics in a box. Pareto-efficiency was the natural, ecological goal of society. All of politics and power relations had to be seen through that lens. History could be seen as the progressive creation of institutions that would minimize the most toxic side effects of conflicts between factions warring over the use of society's resources. But "seen" by who was the question that needed to be asked.

The next wave

THE FIRST TO see the potential application to government in Coase's approach were George Stigler, Samuel Peltzman, and above all Gary Becker. They grafted their theories upon Coase's method to provide an ultimate theory of power.

The irony of their quest was that by using powerful tools from economics and mathematics, these economists arrived, after heroic effort, to the conclusions that Pigou had championed all along. Whether dictated from top-down by government or whether rising from bottom-up by markets and politics interacting, the result was the same. Economies converged, within the constraints of market forces, and the bludgeoning of predators, towards some Pareto-efficient outcome. This brings to mind the old joke about scientists scaling the mountain of knowledge. Once on top they find a group of theologians and philosophers drinking tea and wondering "what took you so long?"

We shall not be drinking this celebratory tea yet but rather exercising ourselves on a long climb. The first serious application of Coasian institutional thinking to the structure of government was undertaken by George Stigler in 1971 in what has become one of the most cited articles in economics. That is not too bad a record for a piece of research that took the recondite method of Coasian reasoning and applied it to understanding what sorts of institutions will evolve to determine how resources are distributed by force. The next chapter shows how Stigler's article became the springboard for what was to become Chicago political economy. This next chapter will be the final preparation we need to understand Becker's formal mathematical model of all power relations between interest groups in society.

Further reading

Becker, Gary S. (1983). "A Theory of Competition Among Pressure Groups for Political Influence." *The Quarterly Journal of Economics*. 98:371-400

Cantor, Norman F. *In the Wake of the Plague: The Black Death and the World it Made*. Harper Perrenial. 2002.

Coase, Ronald H. (1960). "The Problem of Social Cost." *Journal of Law and Economics*. 3: 1–44.

Keegan, John. *The Mask of Command*. Penguin Books. 1987.

Pigou, Arthur C. *The Economics of Welfare*. First edition 1920. Fourth Edition 1932. Palgrave MacMillan. 2013 Kindle Reprint.

Polanyi, Karl. *The Livelihood of Man*. Edited by Harry W. Pearson. The Academic Press, 1977.

Stigler, George G. (1971). "The Theory of Economic Regulation." *The Bell Journal of Economics and Management Science*. 2:3-21.

Temin, Peter (2006). "The Economy of the Early Roman Empire." *Journal of Economic Perspectives*. 20:133–151.

REGULATION 4

T HE PREVIOUS CHAPTER DESCRIBED AN intellectual
spat between Ronald Coase and Arthur Pigou. Coase
thought that Pigou was too fond of prescribing government action whenever markets seemed to fail. Governments
too could fail. You had to compare private with public transactions costs.

Coase started from the remarkable premise that pollution or
any other harmful by-product of commerce was an opportunity for the mutual enrichment of both the polluter and the polluted. Acid vapors that poisoned a farmer's crops were not to
be mourned but rather to be celebrated. If the pollution rights
resided with the farmer then he could charge the firm the costs
of destroyed crops. The firm would adjust pollution-inducing
production to the point where the added cost from the fine to
be paid just exceeded the added profit from extra output of its
poisonous by-product. Both firm and farmers exhausted the
gains from trade to polluting by exchanging cash compensation for the permission to pollute to the point where the value
of extra production no longer exceed the value of destroyed
crops. Even without clear property rights it was possible for
efficiency maximizing deals to be made. Here was Pareto-
efficiency in action, but on a different stage than that envis-
aged by classical economic thinking which took for granted
both bargaining and the institutions which were responsible it.

Coase though was not an apologist for free markets. He acknowledged that his argument for letting the private market take care of harmful "externalities" fell flat if the costs of bargaining, also known as transactions costs, between polluter and polluted were so large that no deal was done. In that case pollution would be excessive and a potential increase in societal wealth from reducing pollution would go unrealized.

Yet the failure of the market to guide people towards mutually beneficial outcomes did not imply that government would be able to do a better job. Governments also faced transactions costs. They needed to invest resources in weighing the claims of both parties. They also had to spend money to ensure that the government will was done. If you accepted Coase's view that transactions costs determined whether Pareto-efficient outcomes could be realized then you could imagine that society would spend resources to devise "institutions" to bring down these costs. Research companies would invent measuring devices allowing farmers to determine the precise level of pollution on their land. An industry in mediation would crop up to spare all parties needless costs of litigation.

Understanding that there was a link between transactions costs and private institutional structure was the "aha" moment that rippled through the orthodox mode of economic thinking developed at the University of Chicago in the late 1950's. Yet few appreciated that this thinking carried over to government.

A decade passed.

Then George Stigler started pushing Coasian reasoning to a new limit. He wanted to show that government power was skewed towards redistributing wealth towards groups in society whose political transactions costs were systematically lower than those of other groups. He also believed that this asymmetry in organizational advantage could be countered by revisions to the way in which power was distributed between different levels of government. That was pure Coasian thinking in action: tracing the line from transactions costs to institutional structure and divining what sorts of investments people would make to lower those transactions costs. His paper failed to close some loops that would have made of it a complete theory of power, but it contained almost all the ingredients necessary for his followers to finish the job.

Our job in this chapter is to clarify the Stigler-Coase view of government. We will have to wait until the next chapter to witness the complete theory. This chapter serves the same sort of function for the total theory of power that the hadiths serve in comprehending the Koran and that Christian critical scholarship serves in understanding the meaning of New Testament. Both Koran and Bible would seem remote and nearly incomprehensible if viewed solely from their foundational texts. The background to understanding the total theory of power needs to be painted here in a similar manner.

First we will ask the seemingly simple question "what is government?" What Stigler had in mind as government is quite different from what most people have in mind. He believed government was strictly a medium through which interest groups contest the control of resources in society. We will see that this view is not wrong, but also risks being overbroad. We will then see that he took the intellectual gamble of being overbroad in his interpretation of government in order to tease out the fundamental features of all governments, be they democratic or dictatorial. Then we will outline how economists thought about government before Stigler came along. We need to do so because much of Stigler's thinking is in reaction to the previous economic orthodoxy on the subject. Stigler's theory has a so-called "positive" aspect, which means that it seeks to understand how transactions costs between interest groups determine the use of power. But the theory also hints at conclusions about the Pareto-efficiency of governments that closely resemble the "normative" way of thinking about the role of government in society.

What is government?

ANY THEORY OF power needs to talk about government. However by the late 20th century scholars from an intellectual school, known today as public choice, began to speak of collective action and choices rather than speaking of government. The reasons are not clear but perhaps they felt discomfort at the ambiguity of the term. This is certainly the theme of Peter Leeson's work on Caribbean pirates. Were they private entrepreneurs in theft, with warehouses, stockyards, and international agreements on the distribution of their stolen goods? Or were they proto-governments with leaders, cabinets, elections? A way of thinking about pirates is as a group of people confronted with challenges that affected them all in a similar manner. Since the threat was collective, one could expect that an efficient response would also emanate from the group.

No matter what the historical period nor the type of collective enterprise being discussed, the defining feature of all collective decisions is that ultimately they rely on mechanisms of enforcement and discernment. Enforcement deals with shirkers, dissimulators, thieves, and other non-conforming parties to an agreement who must be kept in check lest all come to naught. Economists call such people "free riders". When their numbers reach a critical level even normally obedient people decide to lessen their efforts. Brave soldiers are the stuff of myth but they still keep an eye on the ranks to see if desertions are so high that it no longer makes sense to keep one's place in formation. In democracies governments must deal with citizens who cheat on their income tax.

Discernment deals with the problem of knowing what people in the collective wish to achieve. There is rarely a unanimous opinion on all proposed actions. This is seldom a problem for private firms because employees are chosen for their commitment to making money. Those who enforce collective action can forcibly extract money from some to give it to others. People will be tempted to exaggerate their needs. Others will protest. Some will simply try to use the power of government to grab resources from others.

Thus all collective forms of action face transactions costs. Keeping shirkers and tax evaders in line is a costly business. Knowing what your public desires calls for the aid of experts in opinion formation and measurement. These costs in turn determine the form that collective institutions will take. As one can see, by going beyond the simple use of the word "government" one can being to see how Coasian theory may be applied to problems of a collective nature.

A mixed bag

THE JUMP FROM Coasian analysis of private markets to its application in collective action is exhilarating but lands one in a muddied pond. Collective action requires both a means of determining objectives and rousing people to attain them. Unlike in private markets, where no agreement takes place without unanimous consent, collective action, or politics if you will, may deal with opposing interests resolved through the application of force. It also deals with people who share a common interest but who cannot realize it through private agreement. They turn to some collective enforcement mechanism, perhaps government, to impose a coordinated solution in everyone's favor. It is no wonder then that understanding how governments function is harder than understanding how private markets function. In markets, individuals cluster in self-satisfying groups with common goals and beliefs. In politics people may either be unable to cluster to realize a common objective or they may actively exercise force upon each other to nab resources belonging to others.

Yet out of this muddle of mixed-motives some clarity has emerged over the last two thousand years. Cicero distinguished between public interest groups (*partes*) and groups seeking their private interests (*factiones*). Political science taught these practical, descriptive distinctions in first year classes. As we shall see, Stigler viewed these classifications as a physicist might view subatomic particles fused into a larger atom. Stigler thought of power as an extractive relationship between atoms of political interest. Each subatomic unit might follow its own rules, but when fused to others it produced an entity that engendered quite a different theory of power than earlier thinkers had imagined.

The orthodox economic view of government

STIGLER'S EFFORT TO think of political power as the result of transactions costs influencing the formation of interest groups was like a strange animal rooting at the fringes of established economic thinking about government.

The mainstream economist's thinking about government intervention held that government was an instrument for correcting malfunctions in the private sector. The theory on how to correct these blips was there. All that needed to be done was for enlightened leaders to apply it. This theory of intervention-ism had begun with Pigou in the 1920's. He argued that exter-nalities such as pollution could be corrected through a tax or subsidy to bring the market back to a Pareto efficient state. In the 1930's John Hicks and Nicholas Kaldor went a step further to argue that governments could simulate the private mar-ket not just in correcting aberrant prices but also in funding projects in the public interest that for some reason the private market failed to take up. A public road might help some and hurt others but on balance be good for society. Provided the benefit, as measured by the willingness of beneficiaries to pay, exceeded the costs, there would exist a surplus from which losers could be compensated. The process was different from that of a private market but the result would closely resemble the attainment of Pareto-efficiency.

These compensating payments sounded suspiciously like Coasian bargains being struck. This sort of linkage between Pigovian interventionist thinking and Coasian decentralized market reasoning was a long way from being understood. What seemed to be understood was that government could attain Pareto-efficiency through coercion. Here was a truly original thought. Free market thinkers had believed they had a monopoly on Pareto-efficiency. Cost-benefit analysis revealed such thinking to be incomplete. Provided government could provide its coercive services at the same administrative cost as the cost of striking Coasian deals then maximum efficiency would be attained.

The final posts in the Pigouvian edifice were erected by Paul Samuelson and Arnold Harberger in the 1950's. Samuelson showed that markets could also fail by not providing an exotic product he called a public good. It was a gargantuan lapse in the ability of private individuals to roust themselves in public projects benefitting all. Harberger showed that government intervention through taxes created its own special cost known as a deadweight loss. Here was the other side of the ledger. After these architectonic contributions most attention settled on the practical manner in determining how much people were willing to pay for goods which were not transacted in any market. The trick was to infer from closely related private markets the "shadow prices" required for to see if a project was going to be in the black.

Cost-benefit analysis was thus born out of the need to correct market failures. This is simply jargon for prescribing government coercion as a means of mobilizing people to work in their own interests. Cost-benefit analysis held that coercion was the answer to the lack of coordination that was leading to a breakdown of mutually beneficial cooperation. For some reason private institutions were not getting the job done and supposedly government had inferior costs of mobilizing resources and determining what was needed for the public.

Few in the public today understand the lasting legacy of the cost-benefit program for government intervention in the economy. Keynes gets most of the attention as the high priest for dirigisme. Certainly his followers believed that to have been his inclination. But Keynes was a uniquely British intellect upon which labels attached themselves awkwardly. He seemed to some a socialist, to others a conservative. Whatever he was is less easily classified than what he believed. He believed in a government response to social problems that could in part be guided by theory but should also be restrained by the wise counsel of cautious gentlemen such as himself. He had no formal program for government intervention. For that you needed a theory of value. Keynes was perhaps too pragmatic to think he could come up with such a thing. I base these statements on my reading of Keynes' celebrated critique of econometrics as practised by Tinbergen who was one of his admirers. The critique is statistically astute and full of common sense reasoning. It is no way endorses the full scale Tinbergen program of government intervention based on econometric policy evaluation that was to dominate economic policy until the late 1970's. Milton Friedman also gave a televised interview in which he lamented that it was a tragedy that Keynes had died so young. For had he lived, Friedman ruminated, he would have checked the excesses to which his followers pushed his theories.

Cost-benefit economists had no such reticence about government intervention. Their theory of value was based on market economics and a mastery of sophisticated mathematical tools used to calculate the degree of government intervention necessary. Supply and demand were the basic tools of social accounting in the modern world. When markets failed to coordinate people into exhausting all the possible gains from exchange, then a government schooled in the social accounts of supply and demand could set markets right through corrective taxes, subsidies, or outright building programs that coerced people into cooperating with each other in their own interests.

First of the realists

THE PIGOU-HICKS-KALDOR-SAMUELSON-HARBERGER PARADIGM was so powerful and radiated so naturally over all economics that cost-benefit analysis took on the mantle of a "settled science". Economists fully believed their own propaganda about the need for government intervention to restore Pareto-efficiency when markets fail.

They seemed unaware of the Darwinian economic ecology into which they were seeding their ideas. By potentially confusing what ought to be with what actually was, economic advisors could facilitate the very outcomes they sought to prevent.

George Stigler was among the first to point out the dangers of naïve economic policy advice. In 1971 he wrote in his article on regulation "Until the basic logic of political life is developed, reformers will be ill-equipped to use the state for their reforms, and victims of the pervasive use of the state's support of special groups will be helpless to protect themselves. Economists should quickly establish the license to practice on the rational theory of political behavior."

The economists behind cost-benefit analysis had never thought to take out such a license. Doing so would have led them down from the cool esthetic peaks of the differential calculus, upon which Hicks-Kaldor theory was based, to the Coasian lowlands where intuition and a certain form of economic street-smarts reigned. On these streets one compared the costs of different institutional structures to understand how any kind of institution, private, or government, took shape.

To fully understand the contrast in thinking between cost-benefit analysis and Coasian institutional logic, one must mind the tension between idealism and realism. Cost-benefit analysis dealt with what ought to be. The existence of an "ought" implies the existence of an unrealized opportunity. Markets could fail to create wealth that was evidently there for the taking. Governments could pick up what Mancur Olsen famously called "big bills left on the sidewalk", simply by bending over. Coasians admitted that government intervention might be required when markets failed. Markets fail when private agents are unable to coordinate their activities to realize some mutual advantage. The costs of transacting deals that benefits everyone are too high. Yet Coasians warned that governments as well as private markets also faces costs of coordination. Pressure groups interact with politicians to determine how public needs shall be met. Such a complex process of reaching agreement takes effort, negotiation, and in other words cost.

Are these institutional costs low enough to justify the benefits from intervention? That question was never posed in cost-benefit analysis. A Panglossian view of government prevailed. Cost-benefit analysis ignored the processes by which public demands shape policy. This amounted to treating government intervention in the public interest as a free good. Here was a claim worthy of being challenged.

Government as a wealth-grab

THE CHALLENGE TO the view that political action comes without cost came from George Stigler. He wrote that an industry "which seeks political power must go to the appropriate seller, the political party. The political party has costs of operation, costs of maintaining an organization and competing in elections." He was saying that to influence parties that had invested heavily in promoting certain policies you needed to invest equivalent sums to convince them a better way existed. A way that perhaps favored your industry. It was unrealistic to think that a politician or leader would intervene in some group's interest without costly pressures being placed upon her. Whether you belonged to an anti-smoking lobby in California or a human rights movement in Zimbabwe, to gain influence you needed to exert pressure. The tobacco lobby, or leaders of Zimbabwe, would exert contrary pressure. The thrust and counter-thrust of politics costs money. There are no free rides

on the road to optimal or any other sort of government policy. Perhaps this explains why political promises to improve
the public good have little credibility. Such promises imply a
harmony of interest among voters. Since political promises
are so seldom kept, an absence of harmony may be discerned.
The real political world is one of implacably opposed interests
tuned to taking from others to improve their own lot. This
does not mean everyone hates each other. It may equally well
mean that people simply disagree on the means of doing good.

The notion that politics was not a free ride was the more
general part of a sharper critique of government Stigler made
throughout his article. Focusing on a branch of government
intervention known as regulation he suggested that regulation
in the US since the 1930's had seldom served the public interest. Instead, by restricting competition it had kept prices high.
Think of a quota on milk production. By limiting supply the
quota raises prices and enriches farmers. The article became
famous because it had the audacity to subject regulations in
trucking, and professional licensing to empirical analysis sug-
gesting that far from protecting consumers, these regulations
raised the incomes of producers.

Asymmetry in costs

THERE IS NO doubt that casting doubt on the public benefit of
regulations was an audacious, even defiant aim of his research.
Stigler was almost the sole exponent of the view that government was not geared to serving the public interest. The only
other notable like-minded thinkers were Gordon Tullock, who
had started on these lines in 1967 with his article on rent-
seeking. The assumption was present throughout the work of
Mancur Olson in his 1965 opus *The Logic of Collective Action*.

What distinguished Stigler from these fellow travellers was his quest to understand interest group success as a function of the transactions costs of organizing interest groups to influence government. In this sense he was pushing Coase's theory of the firm into politics.

Such thinking was utterly alien in the early 1970's which were still a time when prominent economists admired full-out government control of the economy. Nobel Prize winner Paul Samuelson actively praised the Soviet system of central planning. Even until 1989, when the Berlin Wall was toppling down, the 13th edition of his famous textbook *Economics*, was positing that "The Soviet economy is proof that, contrary to what many skeptics had earlier believed, a socialist command economy can function and thrive."

Yet to those who read Stigler's article closely, its true contribution to political thought lay elsewhere than in the claim that regulation can favor private interests. Its claim to fame lay in being a theory predicting the optimal size of coalitions in politics, showing how economic conditions determined the types of intervention these coalitions favored, and explaining the factors that would mitigate political conflict and lead to economic efficiency. This smacked of a total theory of power.

Stigler's explanation for optimal coalition size lay in the recognition that certain groups in the political contest had an inherent advantage over others. In a very subtle manner he was positing the existence of asymmetries in power. In language familiar to game theorists he specified the conditions of optimal coalition size based on these asymmetries. The search for a theory of coalition size is perhaps one of the Holy Grail's of all social sciences. Asymmetry excites scientists from all fields. Where a fundamental asymmetry exists, distinctions can begin to be made between different constituents of the elements the theory is trying to explain. In physics "symmetry breaking" explains why certain fundamental particles acquire mass. In Stigler's theory of politics, symmetry was broken by differences in the costs of getting different interest groups into action. At the risk of oversimplifying his thoughts, one can state that he believed that in democracies small groups with concentrated interests had an advantage over large groups with diffuse interests.

These aspects of political life may seem obvious but when you push the thought to its conclusion some surprising insights emerge. To compete with the inherent advantage of groups of small size and doted with concentrated interests, large groups may tactically lobby for power to be decentralized. If you can devolve power to the municipal level, small groups lose their advantage, because at that level, everyone belongs to a small group. At the municipal level the problem of coordinating group behavior is not likely to be corrupted by asymmetries in interests. Perhaps Stigler's theory explains the unending tension between state and municipal interests. Certainly it provides us with one possible explanation of the forces forming not only interest groups but also the structure of municipal and state governments. In this sense his theory is in the best Coasian tradition of using the costs of coalition formation to understand the institutional structures we observe.

Asymmetry in gains

STIGLER RECOGNIZED IN passing that when trying to extract resources, small groups also face the problem that their gains from extraction are lower than the costs they impose on their prey. This asymmetry in gains and costs arises from the collateral damage arising from any predatory action. There will always be a certain amount of "wastage" when making off with loot. Economists are more genteel. They use the term "dead-weight loss". Whatever nomenclature one favors, the essence of the matter is that the success of different groups depends on their ability to keep the costs of organizing themselves low enough to counteract the outraged reaction of their targets. Targets feel the pain of extraction more keenly than beneficiaries feel the benefits of their depredations. This inbuilt asymmetry explained why small, powerful groups could not completely expropriate larger groups with diffuse interests. At one point the gain to small groups would be smaller than the loss to large groups and a political equilibrium would be achieved in which extractive activities settled into a fixed pattern.

What Stigler did not twig to was that if victims feel the loss more keenly than predators, then predators have an interest in keeping the collateral damage from their depredations at a low level. In other words, there is an incentive to minimize the damage from political clashes. Thus predatory interest groups may in fact enter into discussions with their victims and negotiate "Coasian deals" that lead to extractive policies that allow some benefit for predators while minimizing the collateral and utterly fruitless damage which may be felt by victims. This deadweight loss is of no benefit to predators. In fact it provokes outrage in their prey. Predators will get the most out of their victims by keeping these deadweight losses to a minimum.

Interaction of economics and politics

WHILE PAYING ATTENTION to the logistics of interest group formation, Stigler's model of politics was at heart rooted in economic conditions. He believed that these conditions determined the form that government regulation would take. If faced with the competitive threat of substitute products, an industry would want to suppress these and encourage the production of complements to its output. As Stigler wrote "the butter producers wish to suppress margarine and encourage the production of bread. The airline industry actively supports the federal subsidies to airports; the building trade unions have opposed labor-saving materials through building codes." The strength of Stigler's article lies in part in the large number of examples he provides to show that the shape of politics is determined by the shape of the market.

Are we all predators?

ACCOLADES SHOWERED ON Stigler for having the gumption to question the public interest theory of government and for presenting an embryonic theory of interest group formation. Yet some questions remained about his approach.

A careful reader of his work had to be troubled by the notion that politics is a combat zone in which government resources are disputed through rival investments by pressure groups. There seemed to be no public interest motive, no nobility in government present in his conception of public life. In a 1976 article that is among the most quoted in economics, Sam Peltzman added to the provocation by inferring that according to Stigler "The essential commodity being transacted in the political market is a transfer of wealth".

Stigler was never quite this explicit. He wrote "political systems are rationally devised and rationally employed, which is to say that they are appropriate instruments for the fulfillment of desires of members of the society. This is not to say that the state will serve any person's concept of the public interest: indeed the problem of regulation is the problem of discovering when and why an industry (or other group of like-minded people) is able to use the state for its purposes, or is singled out by the state to be used for alien purposes." Still, the thought of government as an instrument for redistribution which may or may not serve the public interest is present in the above passage.

The claim that government exists purely to redistribute resources is bound to outrage and puzzle. Yet, viewed logically, the claim is difficult to refute. It follows from the definition of government. Government takes from some and gives to or spends on behalf of others. Those others may include those who pay the bill or may not. No matter what the identity of the recipients and contributors this is what by definition government does. In an otherwise scathing critique of Stigler's research program, Robert Tollison had no problem with the view that in Chicago political economy "… the state is a mechanism which is used by rational economic agents to redistribute wealth. Wealth transfers are the essence of regulatory and governmental behavior in this approach. Governments may, in fact, produce some real goods and services, but these are by-products of effective schemes for wealth transfers."

Bonum publicum emergit ex iniquitate

HOW DID STIGLER assess the autonomous, cynical functioning of government policy that his model predicted? His essay gives conflicting hints. One part argues that regulation serves private interests who "capture" government representatives to serve the industry's purposes. Nothing really good seems to be coming out of this view of the political world. Yet another part of Stigler's essay hints at the possibility of a Pareto-Optimum in politics. Here are the words: "We assume that political systems are rationally devised and rationally employed, which is to say that they are appropriate instruments for the fulfillment of desires of members of the society." The phrase is cryptic but loaded with meaning. It challenges the reader to take up Stigler's embryonic view of politics, as seen through the lens of Pareto-efficiency, and bring it to its logical conclusion.

This bent towards a belief in Pareto-efficiency was due to Stigler's immersion in a school of economics that insisted on three immutable beliefs. Melvin Reder has described these somewhat infelicitously as "tight prior" views. What had to be present for a complete model of any sort of social relation was first the notion that individuals seek what is best for them. The second was that they undertake this quest for self-fulfilment subject to constraints. The third requirement of a theory was that it had to show how individual optimizing decisions coalesced into equilibrium that engaged all other individuals. The definition of equilibrium favored in economics is one in which everyone in society adopts a strategy which, given the assumed strategies of all other people, he or she feels no point in changing. Economists call this Nash equilibrium. Under certain circumstances it can be Pareto-optimal, meaning that resources cannot be reallocated in such a way that at least one person benefits without harming anyone else. Chicago tight-prior was not logically limited to private markets. Its power lay in the presumed ability of its postulates to describe all manner of resource allocations, be they private or public.

Stigler could not quite bring himself to elaborate on efficiency implications of his model. Twelve years had to pass before someone took up the challenge. When Gary Becker published his 1983 paper formalizing Stigler's thoughts and drawing them together in a coherent mathematical model the conclusion was explosive. Subject to certain qualifications, political systems tended not to be wasteful. They might even converge in their outcomes to the sort of results envisioned by the cost-benefit analysts of the 1930's. Out of conflict and violence efficiency in the public interest could emerge. *Bonum publicum emergit ex iniquitate.*

Efficiency also implied that economists should stop giving advice to government. Through the struggles of competing interest groups efficiency had already been attained, though perhaps in a form that was difficult for economists to perceive. Milk quotas, pork-barrel construction projects, trade-destroying tariffs could serve, against every lesson economists had been taught in the classroom, to enhance economic efficiency when perceived against the backdrop of political struggle. How these strange insights arose is the subject of the next chapter, where we tackle Gary Becker's model of power. For now we need to draw together what we have seen of Stigler's first shot at a total theory of power.

Summary

STIGLER DID NOT crank out a complete theory of power. His main interest was in discovering whether regulation was in the public interest. When he discovered the answer was "no" he perceived new dots which he tried to connect. The theory he attempted flapped its wings. Though it was not fully fledged it comprised three key insights that later researchers would fuse into a grander structure.

Stigler's first insight is that government action is not a free good. August personages taking counsel whispered into their ears by messengers from Apollo are not the people we find in charge of government. Real world government agents are subject to interest groups exerting pressure upon them in order to seize control of the public purse or at very least to have a dip at the trough. Inspired by the general Chicago doctrine of "tight prior" Stigler hinted that these conflicts between interest groups might produce policies that could be considered economically efficient. This convergence towards efficiency would have the consequence that economists could forget about giving government advice. An efficient government would have converted all ideas on how to behave efficiently long before an economist had arrived on the scene to notice that some big bills had been left lying on the sidewalk.

The second insight was that two asymmetries influenced the structure of interest groups and the policies they pushed. Small groups with concentrated interests had an inbuilt advantage over large groups with diffuse interests. To the cab driver the loss of restrictions on the number of cabs can mean a reduction of thousands of dollars of revenue. To her fare greater competition between taxis might mean a savings of a few dozen dollars a year. Perhaps this is why a rail line skirts Miami Airport but does not stop there.

Yet small groups, or any group in fact that seeks to feed on others faces the harsh reality that its financial gain will be less than the financial harm it imposes on its victims due to collateral damage. The balance of these two asymmetries determines the structure that interest groups will take, the division of power between levels of government, and the types of redistributional policies undertaken. Redistribution that imposes severe collateral damage will be shunned in favor of more efficient means of extraction.

The third insight was that economic and political structures are deeply intertwined and mutually determining. If a firm such as an aerospace giant has no rivals in its country it will lobby government for direct cash subsidies. Firms with rivals would be better off simply keeping them out, so their best strategy would be to lobby for laws that restrict entry to their industry such as a production quota.

Political parties form in order to create and preserve a brand name that voters can easily recognize. These brand names are especially important to uneducated voters and surprisingly also to voters who earn high salaries and do not have the time to educate themselves on the particulars of party platforms. Parties also form when voters are deprived of alternate instruments for expressing their preferences such as citizens' initiatives. The causality from economics to politics also runs in the reverse direction. Direct democratic instruments lower the cost to citizens with diffuse interests of expressing their preferences. This allows them to better protect themselves against the extractive efforts of small groups with concentrated interests. Thus a country with a strong tradition of direct democracy will also see fewer small economic interests closing markets to competition.

This third point of Stigler's is perhaps his most profound. The joint determination of economic and political structure is a very difficult concept to grasp. It arises from the economist's notion of equilibrium between competing interests. And it is to an examination of this equilibrium to which we turn in the next chapter where we shall examine Gary Becker's effort to unite Stigler's and Coase's thoughts into a coherent and ultimate theory of power.

Further reading

Becker, Gary S. (1983). "A Theory of Competition Among Pressure Groups for Political Influence." *The Quarterly Journal of Economics*. 98:371-400

Coase, Ronald H. (1960). "The Problem of Social Cost." *Journal of Law and Economics*. 3: 1–44.

Harberger, Arnold C. (1971). "Three Basic Postulates for Applied Welfare Economics: An Interpretive Essay." *Journal of Economic Literature*. 9:785-797.

Hicks, John R. (1939). "The Foundations of Welfare Economics." *Economic Journal*. 49: 696–712.

Kaldor, Nicholas (1939). "Welfare Propositions in Economics and Interpersonal Comparisons of Utility." *Economic Journal*. 49: 549–52.

Keynes, John Maynard (1939). "Professor Tinbergen's Method." *The Economic Journal*. 195:558-577.

Leeson, Peter T. (2007). "An-*arrgh*-chy: The Law and Economics of Pirate Organization." *Journal of Political Economy*. 115:1049-1094.

Olson, Mancur. *The Logic of Collective Action: Public Goods and the Theory of Groups*. Harvard University Press. 1965.

Olson, Mancur (1996). "Big Bills Left on the Sidewalk: Why Some Nations are Rich, and Others Poor." *The Journal of Economic Perspectives*. 10:3-24.

Peltzman, Sam (1976). "Toward a More General Theory of Regulation." *Journal of Law and Economics*. 19:211-240.

Pigou, Arthur C. *The Economics of Welfare*. First edition
    1920. Fourth Edition 1932. Palgrave MacMillan. 2013
    Kindle Reprint.

Reder, Melvin W. (1982). "Chicago Economics: Permanence
    and Change." *Journal of Economic Literature*. 20:1-38.

Samuelson, Paul A. (1954). "The Pure Theory of Public
    Expenditure." *The Review of Economics and Statistics*. 36:
    387-389.

Samuelson, Paul A. and William D. Nordhaus. *Economics,
    13th Edition*. McGraw-Hill, 1989.

Stigler, George G. (1971). "The Theory of Economic
    Regulation." *The Bell Journal of Economics and
    Management Science*. 2:3-21.

Tollison, Robert D. (1989). "Chicago Political Economy."
    Public Choice. 63: 293-297.

Tullock, Gordon (1967). "The Welfare Costs of Tariffs,
    Monopolies, and Theft." *Western Economic Journal*. 5:224–
    232.

TOTAL MODEL 5

T HE ULTIMATE GOAL OF CHICAGO political economy was to apply the logic of market competition and equilibrium to the alien context of politics in order to create a total theory of how resources are divided between productive and predatory ends. George Stigler and Sam Peltzman laid the basis for this theory. Gary Becker completed it. The resulting product pits rival interest groups in fights over the fruits of peoples' honest labor. Government may control these resources. Or there may not be a government, only factions fighting over spoils in a civil war.

Regardless of the context to which it is applied, Chicago theory emerges from a world in which people seek to coordinate their efforts towards productive ends. Encroaching upon this world are brigands, thieves, monarchs, tax collectors, special interest groups pleading for congressional favor. In contrast to the world of productive "makers", this demimonde of "takers" destroys resources and discourages productive efforts. It threatens the basis of society. In Hobbes' words "In such condition there is no place for industry, because the fruit thereof is uncertain … no arts, no letters, no society, and which is worst of all, continual fear and danger of violent death, and the life of man, solitary, poor, nasty, brutish, and short." In more prosaic terms, predatory groups represent what economists call a "coordination problem" for society. By identifying the factors that lead to a breakdown in coordination Becker's theory also suggests a path towards re-establishing harmony. Economists call the sort of harmony Becker had in mind "equilibrium".

In economics, equilibrium is a fixed point towards which the behavior of groups of people converges. In markets based on voluntary exchange, this equilibrium is also an optimum for society in the sense that it represents a state in which there are no further possibilities for mutual gain from voluntary exchange. There are no "big bills left lying on the sidewalk" in the words of Mancur Olson. More technically society achieves Pareto-optimality.

These voluntary exchanges are the means by which people fruitfully coordinate much of their behavior in society. To buy a car I need to work to produce income, and to receive this income the seller needs to make an order to the factory where others work, indirectly on my behalf. The coordination is highly decentralized. There is no balloon-brain guiding all actions. It is also efficient in the sense that if there existed a different way to coordinate these actions that left at least one person better off, without harming anyone else, such an opportunity could be exploited without conflict, hence loss of coordination.

If people were to stop exchanging voluntarily and start robbing from each other, a sort of coordination would still exist. It would be the coordination of boxers correlating their footwork to avoid injury while inflicting maximum damage upon their opponents. This violent coordination cannot travel far on its own steam because soon it exhausts all its wealth in combat. Violent coordination needs to draw resources from productive coordination in order to continue its dance of destruction.

Whether applied to an exchange of goods or of blows, equilibrium is the path towards understanding where such contradictory interactions will lead and what the fallout will be. The interactions need not be mutually exclusive. There is an interface and an overlap between the world where people seek productive exchanges and the world in which they prey upon each other. Becker's model joined these two worlds and showed how each influences the other and hence why it makes little sense to speak of "free markets" or "government control" each apart from the other.

Stigler had earlier emphasized how closely linked government and free markets were. Changes in one world could send ripples through the other, as when the great depression of the 1930's saw regimes in Europe and the US forget their liberal traditions and restructure government to command swathes of the economy.

These changes in government in turn forced private markets to become politicized in order to defend their wealth. These political changes further influenced economic change which bounced back to influence change in politics. Eventually a new economic and political equilibrium was reached which lasted through the Eisenhower years in the US.

The extended feedback between politics and economics became the focus of Becker's work. What many saw as a confused interplay of multiple forces, Becker saw as an amalgam of forces that came into focus when seen through the lens of equilibrium thinking. Mastering this thinking is the object of the present chapter.

The objective sounds daunting for a good reason. Economists teach equilibrium in a formalistic manner which obscures how vital the topic is to understanding interactions between people. We might try to take the formalistic route to become masters of equilibrium before exploring Chicago political economy but the effort could prove exhausting and premature. Instead, let us take a bend in the undergrowth of economics and attempt to understand equilibrium with the help of a parable.

The rise of Uber

UBER DESCRIBES ITSELF as a ride-sharing service. It does so to avoid legal battles with taxis. Uber's rise during the age of social networking has provoked outrage in the traditional taxi industry. Its efforts to stifle Uber provide a real-world lesson containing all the elements of Becker's abstract rendition of Chicago political economy.

Over the 20th century coalitions of taxi companies convinced local governments that the number of official permits needed to be restricted. Their public argument for blocking the growth of their industry follows a familiar script with interest groups that are seeking to reserve a market to themselves: riders need to be serviced by companies that meet exacting standards of safety and comfort. Apparently customers are too poorly informed or motivated to make sense of their riding experiences and sift the market for those companies providing desirable features. Only a government issued permit can guarantee consumer welfare. Permits must be limited because the number of satisfactory cabs and drivers is limited.

The subtext to this script is more complicated. Economically valid reasons can be found for having government control the entry of taxis into the market. Yet laws limiting entry, be they passed for taxis, or lawyers, or in agriculture, have the inevitable consequence of raising the price consumers pay above what would be paid in a market with free entry.

Over decades, cab companies were able to impose non-competitive premiums on consumers because of a simple equation governing city politics. The financial interest of cab owners was far more concentrated than that of riders. In some cities the value of a taxi permit could be as high as half a million dollars. This sum reflected the value of the annualized stream of non-competitive premiums resulting from a closed market. An open market would dissolve the value of the permit and lead to the ruin of the owner. To the rider the extra hundred dollars loss of money paid in non-competitive fare premiums is like a mosquito bite in comparison to the cab owner's multi-thousand-dollar non-competitive gain from fleecing hundreds of riders.

This asymmetry in gains gave cab owners a powerful financial incentive to organize themselves into cartels. City governments found it more politically profitable to appease small numbers of drivers by granting them entry restrictions than to care for large numbers of riders suffering from almost subliminal harm. Large gains concentrated on a small group could give it an edge over the masses suffering diffuse losses. Thus taxi policy settled into sort of pastoral calm in which taxis acted like vampire bats, discretely draining cows at night of nearly imperceptible quantities of blood. Here then was a steady state of affairs one might call an equilibrium.

Yet anyone who has studied equilibrium knows that it results from the pull of opposing forces. Concentrated gains gave taxi owners an advantage over riders but there had to be a countervailing advantage riders possessed. Without such an advantage cab drivers enjoying large gains would naturally push for even larger profits. But what if hapless riders suffered more from the additional or "marginal" gain to cab owners than the owners benefitted? In other words, what if a dollar gain to owners resulted in a two-dollar loss to riders? And what if an additional dollar gain to owners pushed the loss to riders up to three dollars? In other words, what if the gains from political pressure were constant for cab owners but the losses to riders ballooned in a manner that is technically known as exponential growth? Clearly in such a case, no matter how passive passengers might initially be, soon they would grumble enough to retaliate against cab owners.

Enter Uber, a private firm with money on its mind and politics in its blood. Noticing the exponential harm non-competitive taxi fares and general neglect of service to customers was creating, Uber decided to become the rider's advocate. The greater loss to riders gave Uber a political edge over cab companies. Consumers could now deal with a new supplier who would help them recoup part of the excessive or "deadweight" losses they suffered from the taxi cartel.

But getting market share by diminishing the harm from excessive fares is not the whole story of how Uber rose to prominence. Harmful fares had been around for decades yet riders had never been able to mount a serious protest against them. As explained earlier, the harm to any individual rider from lack of competition, while annoying, was simply too small to motivate mass protests. In contrast, each cab owner had so much to gain by blocking entry that it was easy for them organize a powerful lobby.

To help riders, Uber could not rely simply on their diluted and dispersed feelings of victimization. It had to find some way to concentrate these feelings in some efficient manner never seen before. The cellphone apps that Uber invented using newly introduced smartphones created the virtual ecosystem in which a community of riders and ride-providers could form at little cost.

This block of newly organized voters awed local politicians into ceding ground to Uber. Some towns have completely allowed Uber to operate, others are struggling to admit Uber into the city's regulatory framework. A few towns, especially in Europe and other countries with feeble democracies continue to deny the legitimacy of Uber. One observes a pattern where prices are falling but not to their free market potential and where the quality of services is increasing. Uber and cab companies fight for political influence but neither is able to completely dominate the other. Both groups tend to settle into some fixed way of existing alongside each other. Call it political equilibrium.

The abstract elements that Becker worked into his model of political interaction pulse in the rise of Uber. Becker was one of the most skilful economic modelers of his generation.

What this means is that he was good at extracting maximum meaning from a minimal number of assumptions about the world. In politics this approach allowed him to produce a model of total power. It encompasses all situations of mass confrontation, be it at city hall or on the marches of empires.

Because the model is built from very general assumptions it is structured to give an answer about almost any political phenomenon. Critics of such models often call them "reductionist". Such models reduce reality to a few simplistic causes and interactions that bear little relation to the complex manner in which the world works.

Fundamental equation a mix of pressure and pain

BOTH SIDES HAVE a point but we can allow ourselves to leave the matter hanging. Ultimately, whether you find the Becker model useful is a question of taste. We can best understand this point by using our knowledge of the Uber saga to delve into the abstractions upon which Becker's model is based.

Our effort to understand political equilibrium will ultimately lead us an assessment of the shocking claim that governments and markets may both converge towards economic efficiency.

Becker's model has several pieces that fit together closely. It has something called variables. For once the technical jargon is understandable. A variable is some quantity that varies, either of its own free will, in which case it is called an independent variable, or under the impulse of some other quantity that is varying, in which case it is called a dependant variable. National income is a dependant variable that changes under the stimulus of independent variables such as consumption and investment.

Other bits in the model are called parameters. They do not vary. Variables and parameters can be joined into something called an equation. On one side of the equation is the dependent variable. On the other are independent variables and parameters that may combine additively, through multiplication, or exponentiation. The possible combinations are without limit. Parameters amplify or diminish the impact that an independent variable has on the dependent variable. So if consumption rises by a dollar, it may have more than a dollar's impact on national income. This impact parameter is known as the multiplier.

The fundamental equation of Becker's model is one which shows how an interest group will react to political pressure and seizure of its resources by another interest group. This is the relay through which all his ideas flow. If you know how cab owners react to Uber and then know how Uber will react to their reaction and so forth, you can see (or "iterate") your way to where relations between the groups might settle down. You can also identify the conditions under which there will be no settling down to an equilibrium.

Two factors determine how a group will react to another. The first spur to action is the group's ability to exert pressure, which is summarized by a "pressure function". The pressure function of cab companies is a mathematical shorthand for their ability to mobilize their members to produce a practical political result. They mobilize with greater ease than riders because each cab owner has a larger money stake involved in preserving her licence than each rider. More generally, a pressure function translates the resources a group spends on political activity into changes in the probability that it will influence the government.

Pressure functions are as varied as the groups to which they pertain. Ease of mobilizing members is just one feature of this function. *Ésprit-de-corps*, cultural similarity, technical savvy, religion, ideology may all help to boost the power of political investments. The pressure function of cab riders was quite feeble until Uber gave them the technical means to act as consumers *en bloc*. The image of riders righteous with the spirit of Uber has shaken politicians. The Uber app is the most important component of their pressure function.

Pain-gain function

THE SECOND SPUR to action is the degree to which a group is either being extorted or the degree to which it may extort resources from it foe. Think of it as the hunger of the wolf or the anguish of its prey. Because the gains of one group reflect, but do not necessarily equal (this is perhaps the key point of this book) the losses of another group, this aspect of Becker's model takes the form of a budget equation that binds both groups. His political budget equation is the most difficult concept in all of Becker's *œuvre*.

At first one is tempted to believe that a predatory group's gains equal the losses that victims experience. After all, if restrictions in cab competition raise the fare by five dollars, it would seem that the cab owner gains five dollars and the rider loses the same amount. Yet in the periphery of this exchange between an individual owner and a rider, an opportunity is being lost. The non-competitive premium is a price hike that discourages some people from taking cabs. Instead, they will seek out less convenient alternatives that come at a lower price, such as riding a bus. These riders suffer from being artificially priced out of an exchange with cab owners.

Economists have developed very specific mathematical tools for calculating the money value of potential exchanges that do not take place because of non-competitive price hikes. They call the value of the lost opportunity a "deadweight loss". The term is infelicitous and largely void of meaning. "Wasted opportunity" would be more fitting. The language is flatulent but the idea is subtle and powerful. It explains why interest groups that have a strong pressure function may falter before seemingly weaker opponents.

The existence of deadweight loss raises the possibility that every dollar cab companies extract in non-competitive premiums provokes, for example, a two- dollar loss to riders, one from the premium and one dollar from the deadweight loss. This asymmetry of gains and losses gives victims a heightened incentive to invest money in their pressure functions, even if these functions are weaker than those of their oppressors. Cab companies may have less incentive to invest in activating their stronger pressure functions because the returns from such investments may be lower than those of their victims. "May" is the operational word in a verbal description that cannot do justice to the mathematical shorthand economists use to describe how people maximize their gains.

We need not be mathematicians to understand what economists are up to when finding out how to maximize the value of a function. How much product a firm should make to maximize profits is among the first lessons economists learn.

Profit is the "maximand" and output is the variable whose "optimal level" we seek in order to maximize profits. If the firm can sell more for a gain that exceeds the cost of producing it, then the firm should increase output. It would be nice to continue on this path but then the problem would have no solution. The firm would keep increasing its output indefinitely while profits tended towards infinity.

The maximizing problem has a solution when the components of profit start changing with each increase in output. Costs are seldom the same for each unit produced. Usually one sees the cost per unit increasing as output increases. Increasing unit costs drive the solution to the maximizing problem. The solution is to increase output until the price of the very last unit produced, the "marginal revenue" comes vanishingly close to the steadily rising cost of providing that extra unit, the "marginal cost". "Marginal" is an economic jargon word meaning "extra" or "additional". Profits reach a maximum when marginal revenues equal marginal cost.

Maximizing the returns from pressure: opening move

NOW WE CAN get a notion of what is going on in Becker's pressure functions. Predators want to maximize money extracted from victims less the cost of doing so. To do this the predator adjusts the amount to invest in the components of her pressure function, such as mobilizing her members to political action. Victims have symmetric objectives. They want to minimize the money they lose and the deadweight loss from the frustration of having to limit their use of cabs less the cost of defending themselves. They too must invest to mobilize their members to beat back the efforts of their oppressors. So how does maximization work here? In the case of Uber, cab owners make an opening gambit. They take political expenditures by riders to be fixed, or "given". That is, they assume no reaction. This is just an assumption Becker makes to get his model going. He modifies it to allow for interest groups to anticipate what their rivals will do, but this does not change the core of his analysis.

Cab owners keep increasing their expenditures on mobilizing themselves for political action until the increasing cost of getting themselves to push even harder for non-competitive premiums just equals the extra or "marginal" gains these extra premiums deliver. The calculation of these marginal gains is based on the cab owners' knowledge of market conditions. Economists call these conditions supply and demand and the equilibrium price and quantity to which they settle.

This is a first indication of how Becker's model blends market conditions and political calculations by a fusion of precise mathematical sub-functions that encapsulate how money is transformed into power and how non-competitive premiums emerge from demand and supply conditions.

Reaction to being preyed upon: countermove

UBER WILL REACT to the opening gambit of cab owners by first calculating how much damage is done to riders, both actual and potential, from the increased political activity of cab owners.

This damage will be greater than the gain to cab owners because of the existence of deadweight loss. But Uber faces a greater cost of organizing riders because their interests are more diffuse than those of owners. Is it possible that these costs inhibit Uber from reacting to cab owners?

Now comes that part that should have been told at the start of this story but would have made no sense to readers if exposed then. The story started by hiding the fact that both groups were already in some stable equilibrium relation to each other. While this is a bit of a cheat, the story cannot be told in any other way without diving into the mathematics. The existence of a previous equilibrium means that Uber had gone through a maximizing process where it kept increasing political expenditures until the increasing costs of political activity exceeded the non-competitive premiums and dead-weight losses kept at bay from predators. Then something changed for cab owners, perhaps in their pressure function, to make it attractive to "re-optimize" by increasing their political expenditures. That "something" which changed could be a new friend highly placed in city hall, or rising demand for cab services. Whatever the reasons for the cab owners' initial thrust, Uber would then react because its marginal costs of organizing had not changed but the benefits from fighting cab owners had increased. Higher takings by cab owners threaten even greater losses to Uber customers. The threat of greater losses increases the gains to Uber of increasing its efforts to beat back newly proposed non-competitive premiums by cab owners. The prospect of increased gain from political activity galvanizes Uber to go through the same process as cab owners. Uber increases spending until the marginal costs once again rise to the level of the marginal gains of political activity.

The story does not end here because it is based on the "Cournot assumption" that neither party believes the other party will react to it. Cab owners all make this assumption and all are surprised by Uber's counter-thrust. So they go back to the drawing board and calculate a new optimal level of political spending, to which Uber then reacts, to which owners react, until either of two things happen. Either both opponents react increasingly violently to each other until political spending continues to balloon without end, or both settle, in ever smaller steps of political reaction to a stable equilibrium. In the first scenario this "game" between opponents is said not to have a solution. In the second scenario the game has a solution in which both opponents see their political spending increase and then stop. Becker believed in the likelihood of the second outcome because of a curious fact about deadweight losses popularized by a mysterious but hugely influential figure in economics named Arnold Harberger.

Non-linearity and equilibrium

HARBERGER DISCOVERED THAT in a demand and supply situation, distortions to equilibrium brought about by artificial price hikes, taxes, and even subsidies, created at first a small deadweight loss, that is, a thwarted or unrealized opportunity for mutually benefiting exchange. Each similar, or "marginal", rise in the distortion created an ever increasing concomitant rise in deadweight loss. Put technically, linear increases in taxes created non-linear increases in deadweight loss.

The non-linearity of any sort of cost should not come as a surprise. When you press harder on the pedal the resulting increase to the speed at which a car is driven leads to ever increasing fuel consumption per unit of extra speed. Non-linearity is a barrier to the expansion of almost all forces in nature.

Becker was the first to understand that the non-linearity of deadweight loss was an important, though not determining factor in the establishment of political equilibrium. If the rise in deadweight loss grows with every increase in tax, then a tax hike will increase the "pain per unit of tax" or conversely the gain from reducing taxes by a unit. In other words, the return to victims from investing in self-defence increases as predators increasingly attempt to grab their wealth. Increasing predation provokes a greater than proportional outrage in the victims. With mounting fury, they redouble their efforts to repulse their oppressors.

Equilibrium comes about as two opposing incentives tug equally at each other. The incentive to mobilize a group to political action is blunted by the rising extra, or "marginal", costs of mobilization. Both predators and prey share this debilitation. What they do not share is the direction in which marginal deadweight losses influence the returns from investing in mobilization. Ballooning deadweight losses raise the returns to prey from investing in their own defence. As prey invest in political influence, predators see their returns from political activity diminish.

Equilibrium comes about when the increasing costs of mobilization catch up to prey and the decreasing returns from extra predation fall to the level of the costs of extra predation. If the costs of mobilization decrease with rising expenses on political activity the picture gets murky and equilibrium depends on some fancy sounding maths that basically state that equilibrium will be attained provided that diminishing costs of mobilization do not overtake rising marginal deadweight losses.

In this arid academic description of humans throwing rocks at each other, Becker glimpsed a bizarre possibility. It seems that rising deadweight loss might give predators an incentive to blunt the harm to victims from their attacks. Becker put it this way "Political policies that raise efficiency are more likely to be adopted than policies that lower efficiency."

On the surface the comment seems to say that Becker believed politics would evolve towards efficiency. We must go below the surface of this sentence to grasp its nuance. For this is the central claim of Chicago political economy. It divides the field from public choice and may drive members of this school to acknowledge that free markets and coercive governments are working towards the same end. Before we can digest this thought an interlude is called for.

A quick summary

LET US CATCH our breath by reviewing briefly the main ideas behind Becker's model of political equilibrium. Until Becker, deadweight loss had occupied a respectable but quiet corner of economics. It was used mainly in the cost-benefit analysis of road and damn construction. Economists were happy to leave deadweight loss in this niche. It did not seem to have any behavioral implications. It was an epiphenomenon of market interactions and government interventions. Its link to social accounting was obscure. No one could conceive of its connection to political behavior. It was the collateral damage from taxation and that was about all you wanted to know on the topic.

Becker thought differently. He saw deadweight loss as the interface between economics and politics. Through that interface he could unite the two fields. His trick for uniting economics and politics was to assume that ultimately the distribution of all resources in society rests upon the threat of violence. All resources in society were up for grabs between rival interest groups. Yes, there was a private market in which people worked together to produced items of value. But on top of this market, government operated by force. The interest group that pushed the hardest was essentially hiring government muscle to back up its play to extract, or extort, rival interest groups. While this assumption might seem simplistic, even gross, it helps to read again the words of the British historian cited earlier in this book. In *The Mask of Command* he writes "But, remote though the battlefield is from the marketplace and the court of law, its pre-existence, or the potentiality of recourse to it, underlie all assumptions citizens make about the order of things as they find them. Force … provides the ultimate constraint by which all settled societies protect themselves against the enemies of order, within and without (pages 311-312)".

The jostle in politics over resources inevitably drains and damages the resource being contested. The deadweight loss that results from tax battles in politics perturbs the market. It represents an upset to the social accounts between people peacefully trading with each other. This upset feeds back into the political world in the form of protests by people who resent paying taxes to subsidize predatory interest groups.

Thus there is a tussle between the creation of value, which takes place in the cooperative setting of the market, and the theft of value, which takes place on the adversarial stage of politics. The tussle between predation and market resistance might go on indefinitely. It might settle into a fixed level of expenditure on political activity by both sides with the concomitant fixed, or equilibrium level of government taxes and transfers.

The endpoint depends on how groups react to each other's behavior. With this quick summary we can now return to asking why Becker thought politics would tend to efficiency and we can examine some historical examples supporting this claim. Though it is beyond the scope of this book, Becker's model also contains insights for competition among lower organisms.

Efficiency of politics

IN STATING THAT "Political policies that raise efficiency are more likely to be adopted than policies that lower efficiency" Becker sowed confusion. He would have done better to qualify this sentence by adding *ceteris paribus.* All other things held constant. These "other things" can overwhelm and negate the efficiency Becker spied sprouting amid conflict between interest groups. He understood this but chose to focus on the one force which no one in economics and politics had noticed nor bothered to assign a role in the theory of power. That force was deadweight loss.

Recall that deadweight loss provokes needless ire in its victims and brings no pleasure to their oppressors. It puts oppressors at a disadvantage. Think of why pick pocketing is almost absent in the US. Individuals from this class of thief pocket the cash and discard the wallet. The thief may gain a hundred dollars. The victim loses a hundred dollars. She also losses documents and financial plastic that can takes weeks of effort to replace. These efforts divert her from living a productive life. They benefit no one. They are a deadweight loss. Due to the asymmetry of gains and losses, outraged victims may thus have a greater incentive to put pressure on the police and politicians than pickpockets have incentive in trying to find new ways of lifting wallets. Deadweight loss may also explain the near total disappearance of mugging in the US. As citizens grow more educated, the value of their "human capital" rises. Mugging is a psychologically and physically violent undertaking. Muggers may cause hundreds of thousands of dollars of damage to the victim's human capital in return for the paltry gain of petty cash. This may explain why muggers are an endangered species, whereas white collar crime flourishes.

Confidence tricksters do minimal physical damage to their victims. They specialize in transferring money from victims to predators with minimal deadweight loss.

The above examples are in the spirit of Becker but stray from his formal analysis. They are not easily quantified in a demand and supply model. But they illustrate why predators find advantage in minimizing harm to their victims. This seemingly benevolent incentive may explain the evolution of taxation.

Becker's model applied to history

BEFORE THE 19TH century taxation in Western countries was a rough business. Governments had not yet developed the bureaucratic expertise to correctly assess the income of its citizenry. Most economic activity could only be taxed by the coarsest of methods. To raise the revenue for their armies, governments allowed their soldiers to be billeted with the population. Peasants frequently revolted against what in effect was a virulent parasitic host of soldiers defining their own revenues through extortion and violence. As civil servants became more expert in identifying regular and non-destructive means of revenue, governments could afford to build barracks in which to effectively imprison their soldiery until they were needed in battle. Deadweight losses of taxation fell. Rebellions of citizens decreased in frequency.

Despite improved methods of detecting income, taxation remained limited to a few obvious sources, such as imports of fine goods and alcohol. Poor citizens hid their money. Rich citizens bribed their way out of paying.

The problem with taxing a narrow base of riches is that the deadweight losses rise at an increasing rate. To keep deadweight losses down and raise more money one must spread the burden over a wide base. Oarspeople driving on a boat understand this phenomenon on a physical level. If one oarsperson reduces her effort the slack must be taken up by others. But the physics of effort is such that for every extra equivalent amount of slack, each remaining rower must expend energy at an increasing rate. As rowers withdraw under the strain, the cooperative effort of moving the boat can collapse. Similarly, governments that rely on narrow sources of revenue face a point of taxation beyond which they risk destroying their base of ratepayers. Thus taxation in Western countries never could exceed roughly ten percent of national income. High deadweight losses from taxation limited governments' fiscal expansion.

Taxation however is not the only means by which government can control revenues. Regulations are a clumsier means of raising money, because they simultaneously entail its expenditure. Despite this shortcoming, if regulations can extract money resources from victims on a broad base they may entail lower deadweight losses than if government taxed and spent the money towards the same end. An example can be found in the minimum wage. Sources of revenue are easily identified: employers of low-skilled labor. By forcing salaries to a level above the market wage, minimum wages take revenue from employers and transfer it to employees. This is a simultaneous tax and transfer of money. The deadweight loss comes from the jobs that the higher wage destroys. According to Becker's analysis, the minimum wage may remain the most efficient and thus popular means of redistributing money if the alternative means of achieving this goal through taxation and spending on the poor provokes higher deadweight losses.

The minimum wage gradually lost its importance as a supplement to income after the second world war. Governments discovered the financial miracle of income withholding. Combined with advances in computer technology, data storage and retrieval, and the emergence of a competent and hard to corrupt corps of tax officials, governments were able to spread income taxes over an enormous base and so reduce the deadweight loss per dollar of tax revenue. The reduction in the collateral damage from taxation led to the decline of redistribution of income by regulatory means and the rise of overt fiscal policies of taxing some to enrich others with direct cash transfers.

The classic article by Vito Tanzi and Ludger Schuknecht (1996), showed that after 1960, the governments of developed countries became feeding troughs. Spending on infrastructure and other traditional government tasks with minimal redistributive consequences faded. Cash gifts expanded. Governments grew in a manner that would have amazed the Pharaohs.

Deadweight and rent-seeking loss are the crux

IN THE CHICAGO school view, the 20th century governments of Western countries grew in part because they could. Falling deadweight losses per dollar taxed, sapped the incentive of ratepayers to resist. This of course is a gross simplification of epic fiscal events and an outrage to those who believe government to be an inherently poor manager of resources.

Becker's model however, when carefully studied, provides a restorative does of nuance. It is true that he believed the fruitless damage from deadweight loss propelled interest groups to seek efficient means of extortion. Yet he also emphasized that the incentive to seek efficiency could be overshadowed by the raw ability of predators and prey to exert influence through their pressure function. If you are really good at imposing your will by force, then rising deadweight costs may not deter you from leaving a trail of economic mayhem in your quest for booty.

Becker was also proposing another loss that had nothing to do with the deadweight losses from takings which were abstractly encapsulated in Harberger's analysis. The second loss was the collateral damage from conflict. When peasants beat their plowshares into swords and go to war they kill one another. They also leave their fields fallow and raid the crops of enemies. To Jagdish Bagwhati, these diversions of talent from producing wealth towards its redistribution "represent ways of making a profit (i.e., income) by undertaking activities which are directly unproductive; that is, they yield pecuniary returns but do not produce goods or services that enter a utility function directly or indirectly via increased production or availability to the economy of goods that enter a utility function. Insofar as such activities use real resources, they result in a contraction of the availability set open to the economy". His term "directly unproductive profit seeking activities" is too lumbering to have been taken up by economists. Instead they use the public choice term "rent-seeking" which is equally infelicitous but seems to have stuck.

The cost of rent-seeking includes the value of all resources thrown into political battle. This is very different from deadweight loss. It is not a by-product of blocked exchanges. It is the direct cost of tussles of over resources. When lawyers flock to capital cities to aid in the fight over a fixed level of resources they generate rent-seeking costs. They could have bent their minds to becoming physicians, carpenters, or pursued any other career in which something new is produced that helps the customer without harming anyone else. That is how wealth gets made. By choosing the mercenary career of counsel to interest groups lawyers impoverish society.

So what is Becker saying?

THE AMBIVALENCE THAT creeps through Becker's model is of the sort that tends to make economists look like wafflers. "Too bad" he would retort. His model started with the simplest assumptions and generated many possible outcomes. The purpose of models was not to nail down absolute truths but to suggest competing views of politics. Which view was right then came down to what the data said. You could not start scrabbling through the data unless you had some idea of what you were trying to find.

Yet something greater than the analysis of mass behavior emerges from Becker's model. By clarifying the issues, he invites us to interpret politics. To Becker the efforts predators make to reduce deadweight losses is a current of efficiency that clearly runs through politics. The efficiency is tainted however because it speeds the path to predatory activities. One could argue that by attempting to reduce the deadweight losses from their takings, predators are cooperating with their prey. Much study has been devoted to deals that conflicting interest groups strike in order to minimize costly conflicts. Romans paid bribes to barbarians to prevent them from plundering. While perhaps avoiding excessive collateral damage these types of interactions can hardly be seen as cooperative exchanges in the spirit of Coase.

A less contrived search for cooperation lies in asking what sorts of constitutions, or rules of the game would induce all parties to limit rent-seeking costs. One such a rule would be to limit campaign spending. Limits would save all parties the expense of buying competing advertisements that only serve to cancel each other out. Such Coasian deals benefit all interest groups. Their evident benefit would encourage a society to embed them in its constitution. Conflicts that cannot be resolved by mutual agreement are left to daily politics

Policy impotence

DESPITE THESE INTERESTING ideas for reform, Becker like other protagonists of the Chicago school is agnostic about the path politics should take to attain efficient use of public resources. In the Chicago view all obvious gains from cooperating in the creation of rules that limit rent-seeking have already been exhausted by competing interest groups. There are no big bills left lying on the sidewalk. Explicit policy advice by economists is likely useless. Governments are behaving as efficiently as they are able under the stresses of competing interest groups. In this manner, governments are implicitly striving towards norms of efficient intervention prescribed by Pigovian cost-benefit analysis.

Summary

ONE OF THE most contentious ideas to emerge from the so-called Chicago school of political economy is the view that all political conflict is nothing but an attempt by pressure groups to grab each others' wealth. This represents a very different form of social calculus from the one put forth by Pareto. He believed that markets would encourage people to exchange their produce until all opportunity for mutually beneficial exchange was exhausted. This provided a form of distribution of wealth that promised societal stability by ensuring that no one would be harmed under the rules of commercial exchange. Markets however have never existed as anything less than an adjunct to governments. Governments by definition specialize in the forced redistribution of resources. Interest groups vie for influence in political battles for the produce created in commercial markets. The social calculus of such predation became the focus of Chicago political economy.

George Stigler who helped found Chicago political economy was astounded that anyone could believe in the benevolence of government, which amounted to believing that government was a free good. Why should we expect valuable resources to be redistributed at no cost to the public in manner that mimicked Pareto efficiency? In other words, why should government be anything but a means by which warring interest groups attempted to divide a fixed pie of public wealth?

Stigler's colleague Gary Becker brought nuance to this stark view in his celebrated 1983 article. He suggested that clashes between interest groups over public resources impoverish society in two manners. Taxes discourage some exchanges from happening between producers and consumers. The value these exchanges would have created is lost to them as well as to society. This deadweight loss is the first harm from political predation. Provided predatory interest groups do not kill the market completely with taxes or other forms of extraction, such as regulations, there is still a fixed pie of wealth to be fought over. The efforts interest groups expend in trying to get their hands on this pie is another waste of resources. Instead using their minds to create new wealth these groups simply dissipate wealth in the contest to grab government booty. These sorts of losses are known as rent-seeking costs.

This dichotomy of costs was well catalogued before Becker by Gordon Tullock in his 1967 paper. But what Becker realised

is that there were forces that could lead to their eventual dimi-
nution. Deadweight costs by definition benefit nobody. That
means predators get nothing out of them. But their victims
become increasingly outraged by every further imposition of
deadweight cost. Drawing on Harberger's analysis of taxation,
Becker noted that deadweight losses suffered by victims tend
to rise exponentially while the tax gains to predators rise only
linearly. This asymmetry of gains and losses meant that victims had a built-in advantage. Their gains from investing in
the political fight rose faster than the gains to their predators
from extracting further dollars. Intelligent predators would
then seek to extract resources by means which minimized
deadweight losses. This is why Becker felt politics could tend
towards efficiency.

What about that second cost, the one called rent-seeking?
Becker said you had to think of deadweight and rent-seeking
costs as being determined at two different stages of a political
"game". The first stage, call it a constitution, takes place before
the game starts. Players agree on rules of the game that would
lessen the dissipation of their resources in the contest for government favor. Becker mentioned rules that limit campaign
spending as an example of a pre-game rule that holds down
rent-seeking costs. In the second stage, call it elections, the
game starts and groups begin to look for ways to extort money
from others. The most successful will be those who keep down
their deadweight costs.

What Becker was saying in a more general sense is that the
quest for Pareto-efficiency can be present even in a non-coop-
erative setting such as politics. This quest attenuates the worst
excesses of predatory groups. Because these groups ultimately
rely on the threat of government force to get their way, the
search for lower deadweight costs can be thought of as the

search for a "better kind of violence". But this efficiency and lessened violence are tainted. They are the by-product of a conflict to divide resources which ultimately impoverishes society.

What is most fascinating in Becker's article is the manner in which it merges supply and demand, good traditional economic concepts, with political concepts such as functions that show the return to spending money on lobbying. Such a merger of ideas allows the reader to speculate on the future of the world.

During periods of great market flexibility, such as we saw for two hundred years leading up to the last quarter of the 20th century, the deadweight losses from taxation were bound to be very large. Flexible or "elastic" demand and supply mean prices and quantities react sharply to disturbances such as taxes. Thus there is a strong incentive for potential prey to protect themselves from predators. Markets were allowed to function freely and wealth exploded in a manner never before seen. The article by Tanzi and Schuknecht shows how taxes never rose above ten percent of GDP in the 19th century.

If demand and supply become rigid, say through the application of constraining regulations that limit competitive entry to the market, then people cannot flee taxes by going to other markets. Thus the tax does not discourage exchanges and deadweight losses are small. But small deadweight loss robs victims of their inbuilt advantage. The field now becomes dominated by predators who fixate on dividing the fixed spoils found in the market. The advantage of predators is that they have excellent "power functions". They are good at taking as Mancur Olsen elaborated in his *The Logic of Collective Action*. This society of rigid markets and broadening rent-seeking gradually impoverishes itself. Can this be why per-capita incomes in the west have either stopped growing or shrunk? Will such a deviation from Pareto efficiency upset the accounts that keep society unified? Chicago political economy may not have the answers, but it provides a slide rule for helping to calculate them. Of course, not everyone agrees, and to these skeptics we now turn in the following chapter.

Further reading

Bhagwati, Jagdish N. (1982). "Directly Unproductive, Profit-Seeking (DUP) Activities." *Journal of Political Economy.* 90:988-1002.

Becker, Gary S. (1983). "A Theory of Competition Among Pressure Groups for Political Influence." *The Quarterly Journal of Economics.* 98:371-400

Coase, Ronald H. (1960). "The Problem of Social Cost." *Journal of Law and Economics.* 3: 1–44.

Harberger, Arnold C. (1971). "Three Basic Postulates for Applied Welfare Economics: An Interpretive Essay." *Journal of Economic Literature.* 9:785-797.

Keegan, John. *The Mask of Command.* Penguin Books. 1987.

Olson, Mancur. *The Logic of Collective Action: Public Goods and the Theory of Groups.* Harvard University Press. 1965.

Olson, Mancur (1996). "Big Bills Left on the Sidewalk: Why Some Nations are Rich, and Others Poor." *The Journal of Economic Perspectives.* 10:3-24.

Pigou, Arthur C. *The Economics of Welfare*. First edition 1920. Fourth Edition 1932. Palgrave MacMillan. 2013 Kindle Reprint.

Stigler, George G. (1971). "The Theory of Economic Regulation." *The Bell Journal of Economics and Management Science*. 2:3-21.

Tanzi, Vito and Ludger Schuknecht (1996). "Reforming Government in Industrial Countries." *Finance and Development*:2-5.

Tullock, Gordon (1967). "The Welfare Costs of Tariffs, Monopolies, and Theft." *Western Economic Journal*. 5:224–232.

PUBLIC CHOICE   6

THIS CHAPTER EXPLORES THE VIEWS of a school of
thought, known as public choice, which has been a stern
critic of Chicago political economy. Both schools share
the methodology of applying economics to political phenomena. Both view politics as consisting of politicians (often call
"agents" in the economic jargon) and their subjects (often called
"principals"). Both groups seek to maximize their own welfare,
subject to monetary and constitutional constraints. Chicago
believes that political competition creates efficiency in government by aligning the interests of agents and principals and that
this efficiency emerges no matter what the political context nor
the advice governments receive from experts. Dictatorships,
oligarchies, democracies all converge to efficiency and there is
no point in having academics either encourage or discourage
this tendency. It happens independently of intellectual mus-
ings. Public choice believes that there are powerful forces pre-
venting the emergence of political efficiency and that academics can influence its emergence.

Background to a conflict

CHICAGO POLITICAL ECONOMISTS wish to encapsulate in a
consistent, mathematical form, a unified model of politics
and economics. Their central conclusions are that a society in
which people seek their own wellbeing converges toward an

efficient equilibrium. Economists can study and model this spectacle but because efficiency is woven into human behavior, armchair advice from professors dabbling in public policy is superfluous. People do not leave large bills lying on the sidewalk. Mancur Olsen wrote in 1996 that if these ideas

> ... are largely true, then the rational parties in the economy and the polity ensure that the economy cannot be that far from its potential, and the policy advice of economists cannot be especially valuable. Of course, even if economic advice increased the GDP by just 1 percent, that would pay our salaries several times over. Still, the implication of the foregoing ideas and empirical assumptions is that economics cannot save the world, but at best can only improve it a little. In the language of Keynes' comparison of professions, we are no more important for the future of society than dentists.

Not everyone agrees with Chicago political economy. Public choice, which has evolved in parallel contains a faction, known as the Virginia school, and a sub-faction known as constitutional political economy. Its members cannot not help but think of Chicago with repugnance. Charles Rowley, editor of the *Encyclopedia of Public Choice*, captures the general sentiment in the following excoriation:

> When Gary Becker (1976) remains willing to defend in-kind transfers as carrying lower excess burdens than lump sum transfers of income, when George Stigler (1992) argues that all long-lived trade protection tariffs are efficient, while William Landes and Richard Posner (1987) defend U.S. tort law as being economically efficient, and while the Journal of Political Economy publishes papers that defend the U.S. federal farm program as an efficient mechanism for transferring income to poor farmers, there is justifiable cause

to worry whether CPE scholars and their journal editors ever look
out from their ivory towers and survey the real world.

Warming to his theme, Rowley concludes "Specifically,
Becker suggests that interest groups redistribute wealth efficiently, minimizing the deadweight costs to society. Groups
that impose high deadweight excess burdens, in this view, are
replaced by more efficient alternatives. This Panglossian view
has its advocates, mostly from the University of Chicago. The
public choice evidence almost universally refutes the predictions of the model."

We have studied the Chicago school in depth in previous chapters. What is this public choice school that calls into
question Chicago's central conclusion of tendencies towards
efficiency in politics? The reasoning and methods of the two
schools are so similar that to an outsider disagreements seem
contrived. The difference arises not so much in the tools used
by both schools but rather in a metaphysical posture.

Chicago scholars see models as impartial means for making sense of a jumble of facts. Within data lie behavioral relationships such as the manner in which people react to prices
and changes in their incomes. These may sound like trivi-
al pursuits until one realizes that from an understanding of
these fundamental reactions a comprehensive picture of the
economy emerges. Chicago's belief in market efficiency under-
cuts the notion that economists have anything useful to say to
governments.

Public choice scholars view themselves as integral to the
models they formulate. To them ideas matter. It is the role
of the public choice scholar to inject these ideas into politics as inoculation against harmful policies. Their most complex and important assertion is that politics should be seen as

a two-stage "game" between coalitions of voters. The second stage of the game is politics as most people know it: elections, lobbying, interest group competition. To keep down the conflicts in this second stage, a polity should have a first stage in which a constitution is written which limits the size of government. People will then find it more profitable to focus on voluntary market exchanges as a way of determining resource use.

Public choice scholars, especially those adhering to a branch of the field called constitutional political economy, believe that it is during the first stage of the political game that scholars can make their influence felt. They are ready to concede that during the second stage, the chance for scholarly influence may be small because at that stage the pressures of constant competition render the individual irrelevant.

To understand this striking way of reasoning let us then examine public choice to see what its ideas about competition and political efficiency are.

Public Choice

PUBLIC CHOICE IS based on the median voter theorem. The theorem holds that in political equilibrium parties will follow the wishes of the "median" or middle voter.

Take a room with a hundred and one people and ask them what their desired level of government spending is. Arrange them in a line starting at one end with those wishing the lowest level of spending to those wishing the highest at the other end. The fifty first person in this identity parade has fifty people to her left and fifty to her right. She is at the "center of mass" or median of the distribution of people arranged by their preferences. Her preferences are those around which parties will shape their platforms.

In 1929 Harold Hotelling solidified this notion in his article on where firms would locate to be closest to customers. It makes no sense for each owner of two ice cream stands to locate at far ends of the beach. If one locates at the left end the other can nab all customers by coming between her and everyone to the right of her. To keep customers, she will move her stand just to the right of her competitor. Both will keep leapfrogging each other until half the potential customers are on one side of each stand. Similarly, parties "located" on a left-right political spectrum will avoid extremes and apply the logic of ice cream stands. Move to the center to nab the most voters.

The rush to the center produces a political equilibrium based on the optimizing calculations of parties and of voters. In 1948 Duncan Black reproduced Hotelling's result without citing him. In 1957 Anthony Downs reproduced the Hotelling result, citing Hotelling but ignoring Black. This sort of selective memory in citation is normal business in academia, perhaps because few people care about intellectual history and just want to get to the result. The result is now widely known as the median voter theorem.

The median voter theorem is more specific than Becker's equilibrium model of politics because it posits a spectrum along which policies are formulated, and makes some detailed assumptions about voter preferences such as "single-peakedness" which need not concern us.

This more focused picture of politics in no way contradicts Becker's model. Instead, the median voter model can be seen as a subset, or one possible manifestation, of equilibrium that fits into Becker's all-encompassing formulation of that concept. The fact that one model snuggles inside another alerts us to the possibility that long before the Chicago school, notions of efficient political equilibrium were stirring.

Stirrings of political equilibrium and efficiency

IN THE 1940's and 50's when the concept of political equilib-rium was just beginning to emerge, little thought was given to its efficiency. The best brains in economics at the time, such as Lionel McKenzie, Kenneth Arrow, and Gerard Debreu were struggling with proving the efficiency of economic equilibrium. Düppe and Weintraub describe this quest in their 2014 book *Finding Equilibrium*. Political equilibrium and its implications for efficiency were still undeveloped concepts. Yet something political stirred at the fringe of economics.

In 1954 Paul Samuelson ventured into the then nascent field of public finance economics. He asked whether the rules of free markets could apply to governments. The answer was no. The sole economic justification for government at that time was that it should provide "public goods". Private markets would not produce enough of such goods because they were "non-excludable". You could not prevent someone from con-suming them.

Streetlights are an example. How do you charge someone for enjoying the safety of walking down a lit street? The non-excludability of lighting explains why most cities went unlit until the mid-nineteenth century.

Private suppliers would not produce lighting because they could not charge for it. Charitable suppliers could not pro-duce lighting because of the problem of free riding. Some good souls might contribute to a street-lighting fund, but others would simply not pay and coast on the efforts of others. Such ventures generally founder, despite an important truth. It is to the benefit of all, except perhaps cat burglars, that streets be lit. Yet without the means to enforce payments, a project that benefits all goes unrealized. This lack of coordination between members of society creates a Pareto inefficiency. Enterprises of great public value never see light.

To produce such "non-excludable" goods society needs a system of forced payment. It is called taxation. Such a system must itself be efficient. If government takings destroy the economy, there is no value in producing public goods. It was only around the mid-nineteenth century that western governments figured out how to extract resources from their subjects efficiently. This efficiency allowed governments to ponder the other side of the decision ledger, which is, once you decide a non-excludable good can be financed at some reasonable cost, what level of such a good should you provide?

Economists have a ready answer to such questions. Benefits net of costs are maximized when the marginal benefits and costs equal each other. In economics, as in mathematics, marginal means extra. A project should be carried to the point where the added benefit of spending an extra dollar on it just equals the added costs. If the added benefit is greater then more should be spent. If it is lesser, then less should be spent. This decision rule can only be of practical use if governments know what a project costs and the benefits it brings.

Knowing cost is simple, but not as simple as you might imagine. There is naturally the direct dollar cost to consider, but each dollar of taxation discourages economic activity. The value of discouraged activity is known as deadweight loss.

The benefits of a project are generally harder to divine. Governments seeking to maximize Pareto efficiency must push production to the point where the extra amount that the sum of people in society is willing to pay, equals the cost.

We do not need to get into peoples' heads to scan how much pleasure they get from something. Pareto efficiency is concerned strictly with unexploited opportunities. People demonstrate their willingness to pursue these opportunities through their willingness to pull money out of their pockets.

But how much money will people pull out for non-excludable goods? This is a hard question because there are no markets for non-excludable goods. Thus we have no idea of how much extra money people would be willing to pay for more of the product. The answer lies in an egg-hunt for market data of similar goods but which are excludable, and need not concern us here lest we embark on a distracting detour from the story of political equilibrium and efficiency. The point is that there are imperfect means of calculating the marginal benefits and costs of providing non-excludable goods. But knowing how to calculate these costs and benefits did not satisfy economists that they could devise a rule for optimal government intervention where markets failed.

The rule economists finally settled upon arose from a mysterious obsession they nurtured in the 1950s. For some reason, economists came to think of public goods of as possessing a second feature in addition to non-excludability. The infelicitous term for this second feature was "non-rivalry" in consumption. Public lighting is non-rivalrous because my enjoyment of this lighting does not detract from anyone else's enjoyment. A sandwich is rivalrous because the bite I take is usually no longer available to others.

Non-rivalry was not a necessary justification for government intervention. Movie theatres provide a non-rivalrous product but manage without government aid because they are able to keep away non-paying viewers. Only non-excludability is a justification for government's intervention to push an economy to the frontier of Pareto efficiency. Perhaps economists of the time believed that non-rivalry and non-excludability were inseparable.

In his essay on light houses Ronald Coase gives some idea of how people were thinking at the time. Let us not quibble. Our quest is to understand how Paul Samuelson's result on the optimal provision of public goods ignited the fusion of thought on political efficiency and equilibrium.

Samuelson's result

SAMUELSON SOLVED THE problem of the optimal provision of public goods by recognizing that a non-divisive good brings some benefit to each person each time the quantity of the good is increased. This extra or "marginal" benefit may vary from person to person. To get the optimal level of public good one simply had to keep increasing the level of good until the money and deadweight loss cost of the tax to finance this marginal quantity equalled the sum of marginal benefits to all who received non-rivalrous benefits.

The result interested economists in the field of cost-benefit analysis, but it had a broader significance than that imagined by social engineers seeking a mathematical formula for optimal government intervention. Samuelson's result could be wedded to the fundamental equilibrium concept of public choice called the median voter theorem. The child of this wedding would be the first ever formal proof that politics could be Pareto efficient.

The proof of this assertion is disarmingly simple. The median voter theorem posits that parties will offer a platform appealing to the median voter. The median divides people on the left equally with people on the right. If public opinion is distributed evenly from left to right on some index of issues, then the median is also the average of opinions. But what is an average other than a sum, divided by the number of individuals being counted? Samuelson's theorem says that the optimal level of public goods is determined by the sum of marginal benefits received by the populace made equal to the marginal tax cost. One can divide both sides of this equation by a constant, such as the number of people and still obtain the same optimal level of public goods. The average marginal benefit however is also the benefit coming to the median voter. Thus on one side of the equation one can forget the preferences of all voters except that of the median voter. Hence the median voter's preferences, balanced against the tax cost of providing the public good determines the optimal level of government intervention in the economy.

The efficiency of government in a society where the median voter rules emerged decades ahead of Becker's fusion of economics and politics. The notion of public goods was still too fresh to be widely known. The concept of political equilibrium was barely fledged. The academic world was not ready to appreciate the Black-Samuelson synthesis in which political efficiency of the rule of the median voter were fused.

Not until the mid-1970's did economists start pondering this result. They came from the public choice school, which at that time held government to be inherently inefficient. Charles Rowley explained: "If problems of monopoly, externalities, public goods and bounded rationality afflicted private markets, they simply ravaged political markets that confronted individuals with massive indivisibilities and severely limited exit options."

They need not have worried too much. As Dennis Mueller explained in this 2003 survey of public choice "the sophistication and elegance of the theoretical models of public choice far exceed the limits placed by the data on the empirical models that can be estimated". What this means is that to get empirical support for your theory you need data that vary sufficiently in order to reveal relationships between dependant and causal variables. Efforts to validate the median voter model focused on trying to show that government spending in a political district is more closely wedded to the income of the median voter than it is to the income of the average voter.

The data do not show enough variation to allow the dominance of median income as an explanatory variable to be discerned. The median voter may determine the level of government spending, but conclusive evidence is still being vigorously debated. Most importantly, we cannot conclude that politics leads to an efficient provision of public goods in the narrow Black-Samuelson sense because we must still proceed with caution when arguing that equilibrium is determined by the median voter.

A summary of differences

OUR TOUR D'HORIZON of public choice explains why it opposes the notion that political competition leads to government efficiency. The data do not give any consistent support for this notion. This is what one would expect if one accepts the public choice view that competition is difficult in politics because of voter ignorance and powerful barriers to competition that power-seekers put in place.

The Chicago riposte to this critique is that competition must be viewed as taking place within unalterable constraints. Chicago admits that voters choose to be selectively ignorant because it does not pay to be fully informed. Only one party may rule at any given time and is thus shielded from the simultaneous offering of competing government products by political rivals. Other facts such as the large fixed costs of attaining power create barriers to entry into politics. But there is no point in whining about these realities. They are constraints.

Everyone maximizes their wealth within constraints and that is the best we can do. Mainstream economists may say that the minimum wage is an excrescence from politics that creates unemployment. Chicago would say that, yes, this may be so, but if the minimum wage exists to transfer income to the poor, it does so because other means of transferring income, such as through taxation and direct subsidy, create greater deadweight loss. To push the point to its extreme, Chicago would give a nuanced answer if asked to judge the Meso-American practice of human sacrifice. To us such behaviour is shocking. But it may have been a method to control population growth that avoided the deadlier alternative of civil war due to excessive competition for the control of nutritive resources.

No one summarizes the Chicago view better than 18th century poet Alexander Pope. In his *Essay on Man* he wrote "All Nature is but Art, unknown to thee; All Chance, Direction which thou can'st not see; All Discord, Harmony not understood; All partial Evil, universal Good: And spite of Pride, in erring Reason's spite, One truth is clear; "Whatever Is, is RIGHT."

The Chicago argument for political efficiency maddens public choice scholars. They suspect themselves trapped in the vise of a sophisticated tautology: in politics only the most efficient outcomes will obtain because the human effort to leave no opportunities for the creation of wealth unexploited leads to efficiency. The tautology lurks in the phrase "the human effort to leave no opportunities for the creation of wealth unexploited". This can be logically equated to meaning that "human effort leads to efficiency". Thus the Chicago proposition could be restated as "in politics only the most efficient outcomes will obtain because the fact that human effort leads to efficiency leads to efficiency." The evolution of species by natural selection of the fittest and Freudianism provoke similar irritation in their critics.

Despite their ire at the Chicago view, public choice scholars quickly learned to play a similar game. In his 1982 essay on the Chicago school, Melvin Reder called this game "tight prior". You build up a theory on the basis of ideology. There is no such a thing as letting the facts speak for themselves. There are too many facts to make sense of them by sifting them. You have to assert your view of the world and see if the facts go along (some people call this putting on rosy glasses). Chicago believes that equilibrium prevails in economic and political markets and that this equilibrium is Pareto efficient. Contrary evidence is not particularly welcome. As Reder writes "Any apparent inconsistency of empirical findings with implications of the theory, or report of behavior not implied by the theory, is interpreted as anomalous and requiring one of the following actions: (i) re-examination of the data to reverse the anomalous finding; (ii) redefinition and/or augmentation of the variables in the model." Along this line, government efficiency is difficult to measure as is political competition. Until such reliable measures come along it will be difficult to reject the tight prior view that political competition leads to government efficiency.

Given the challenges of finding conclusive evidence on the link between competition and efficiency, public choice scholars are free to put forth their own tight prior. Yes, competition in politics may lead to economic waste from "rent-seeking"; the efforts expended on dividing wealth rather than on creating it. Yet this is not an unalterable optimum as Chicago maintains. Public choice scholars can give advice to move politics towards greater efficiency. These scholars do not sit outside politics but rather are an organic part of it. They play a decisive role in determining the course of society.

In the vacuum of decisive empirical evidence, the argument between Chicago and public choice appears to be a metaphysical debate going back to the time of Plato. Do we have free will? Chicago seems is obdurate in its "no". Public choice says yes, but in a subtle manner that poses a significant challenge to Chicago thinking.

Enter Buchanan and Brennan

IN THEIR 1977 article *Towards a Tax Constitution for Leviathan* Nobelist James Buchanan and Geoffrey Brennan argued that conventional economic thinking about the rules that should govern optimal government intervention were blinkered. Conventional thinking imagined either a benevolent social planner, or a political system geared towards the wishes of the median voter. In such a system governments would levy taxes that minimally discouraged the creation of wealth and would spend only to the degree that public goods were provided optimally for the populace.

Buchanan and Brennan rejected this idyllic view. They feared that government would ignore economic notions of optimality and instead suck as much tax as it could from its subjects. The growth of a government "Leviathan", a mythical beast rising from the ocean to devour ships, would then lead to all sorts of abuses of power. To contain Leviathan, they argued that politics should be seen, in the fashionable jargon of the time, as a "two-stage game".

In the first stage a constitution would limit the abilities of government to tax. With Leviathan thus contained, a second stage could then be played in which political competition could nurture efficient economic outcomes.

Political competition might severely restrict the ability of scholars to influence policy in this second stage. The scholar was at his mightiest in the first stage where all founders of the nation recognized their mutual interest in getting right the rules of the political game. In the search for such truths scholars could be of great help.

Thus public choice tacitly acknowledged some of Chicago's ideas about political competition and efficiency (second stage of the game), while at the same time finding a role for the scholar to influence policy (first stage of the game). From these insights the branch of public choice known as constitutional political economy was formed.

Efficiency through inefficiency?

THE ONLY BLEMISH on Buchanan and Brennan's foundational essay was their rejection of public choice's core belief in the median voter model. With a flick these fathers of the field dismissed what at the time was the only fully worked-out, logically consistent formulation of political equilibrium. Instead, they based their argument on a new and largely untested notion of the "budget maximizing bureaucrat" put forth by William Niskanen in 1971. Buchanan and Brennan's gambit showed how easy it is to sneak in prejudices against big government by abandoning the discipline imposed by models of political equilibrium. The dangers from "Leviathan" were not based on a model, but rather on a personal conviction.

Yet it would not be productive to dismiss Buchanan and Brennan because of their recourse to an intellectual *deus ex machina*. They were tracing the outlines of a profound thought but lacked the theoretical tools and insights to make it stand on its own. The appearance of Becker's 1983 article on interest group competition suggested that the Leviathan argument had legs. It was consistent with Becker's model of political equilibrium, but in a very particular sense.

In the Buchanan and Brennan article Leviathan will attempt to maximize government revenues. To limit Leviathan, constitutional restrictions on the ability to tax must be passed in order to lower revenues governments can extract from the economy. In Becker's model a restriction on available "tax instruments" works not by limiting the maximum that can be raised but by increasing the deadweight loss imposed by taxes. Being an equilibrium model of politics, Becker's model postulates no tendency for government to maximize its revenues. Instead it neutrally postulates that voters will consider the direct and deadweight costs of taxation in determining the level of political pressure to exert. One cannot really speak of demand and supply in this model, but rather of the final, equilibrium levels of pressure different groups decide to exert on government given the tax plus deadweight cost of different policies.

A prediction of the model is that more of a service will be provided the lower is the deadweight cost associated with its provision. Becker and his colleague Casey Mulligan found empirical proof of this in 2003. It seems that countries with more efficient tax systems, those imposing less deadweight loss per dollar of tax, also have larger governments. Thus one could restrict the size of government by writing a constitution that only allows government to use inefficient tax instruments. By raising the deadweight loss from taxation interest groups seeking government favours would find themselves disadvantaged in the face of those seeking to resist having to pay more tax.

Yet why exactly would one wish in the Becker model to restrict anything? It is after all a model predicting the possibility that political competition may lead to the economically efficient provision and financing of government services. The model emerged from the best tradition of Chicago optimizing behavior. Why mess with the human behavior it predicts?

The answer lies in a collateral damage from politics known in public choice as rent-seeking, and in some other academic quarters as directly unproductive profit-seeking activities. When a society's best and brightest devote their energies to carving up the nation's wealth rather than figuring out ways of increasing it resources are squandered. Every dictator who spends half his country's GDP to protect his position might have had a career as a scientist or an architect had the rules of the political game discouraged rent-seeking.

So how does rent-seeking enter into plans to restrain Leviathan? As Becker and Mulligan had verified, a political system that minimizes the deadweight loss from taxation encourages government to grow. The resulting large government attracts what historian William McNeill called human macroparasites who do battle to control government resources. If the tax system were inefficient, interest groups would have a weak incentive to demand a large government. The cost of increased inefficiency might be more than balanced by the resources saved from discouraging the non-productive efforts that macroparasites expend in their quest for government booty.

So who wins?

As THIS CHAPTER must by now have made clear, the claims of Chicago political economy oppose those of public choice.

Detailed examination reveals that both schools of thought agree on the tools needed to analyse politics. Individuals are assumed to maximize their well-being subject to material constraints and the result of these activities will produce an equilibrium. The schools differ in that Chicago sees political equilibrium as being Pareto-efficient and beyond the power of an individual to influence. Public choice believes that inefficiencies in the political market prevent the emergence of efficiency and that the scholar can change history. Neither school can as yet be proved to have the better argument because the data needed to verify claims about competition and efficiency in politics are scarce or entirely missing.

Is there any middle ground between these two schools of thought that might begin by acknowledging the inefficiency of political equilibrium, but that might also suggest some credible means of overcoming this inefficiency? The answer will satisfy neither Chicago nor public choice. It is called mechanism design, a field which emerged from game theory and which some call anti-game theory.

Game theory

GAME THEORY IS a copious wonderland of imagined equilibrium relations between rivals. Remember what equilibrium is, a stable set of relations between individuals or groups of people. Standard economics works mainly on the unique equilibrium that can be found at the intersection of demand and supply curves. Game theory may now have uncovered dozens of fundamentally different types of equilibria and continues to produce them. In many ways it is similar to quantum physics where new particles emerge from ever deeper theories. That is no idle coincidence. The rule of particle physics is unpredictability. Games theory also has trouble pinning down how rival individuals or groups will resolve their conflicts. The closer scientists peer at the individual components of nature, the less they seem able to say about their behaviors. Yet in this embarrassment of riches, game theory may provide just the sort of insight which could unite Chicago and public choice thinking, though not necessarily in a manner that either school would approve of.

Though game theory is now a recognized field of economics, most economists shy from it. That is no surprise. Game theory was created by mathematicians who had little point of contact with economics. Their views on equilibrium turned out to be so weird and ran so obtusely against intuition that economists ignored the field for decades. To understand what game theory is we must first understand what it is not. Nobelist John Harsanyi explained that

> In principle, every social situation involves strategic interaction among the participants. Thus, one might argue that proper understanding of any social situation would require game-theoretic analysis. But in actual fact, classical economic theory did manage to sidestep the game-theoretic aspects of economic behavior by postulating perfect competition, i.e., by assuming that every buyer and every seller is very small as compared with the size of the relevant markets, so that nobody can significantly affect the existing market prices by his actions. Accordingly, for each economic agent, the prices at which he can buy his inputs (including labor) and at which he can sell his outputs are essentially given to him. This will Games make his choice of inputs and of outputs into a one-person simple maximization problem, which can be solved without game-theoretic analysis.

In other words, classical economics has no need of game theory because it forces the individual to accept the constraints imposed upon her while deciding how to maximize her well-being. In game theory the constraints are more fluid.

A person placed in game-theoretic interactions seeks, as in the standard economic analysis, to maximize some objective. But she is not like the consumer of products who must passively accept the constraints imposed upon her by the economic environment. In game theory, the constraint lies in the opponent's mind. That mind will conceive a strategy based on its anticipation of one's own strategy. This means that one's own mind is shaping to some degree the constraints one faces. Unlike the passive consumer taking prices and making choices, in a game a person's choices can influence her possibilities. She is forced into a "strategic interaction" with her environment. She does not choose the outcome, but rather a strategy that may or may not produce the outcome she wants. By taking charge of her environment she also determines in large part what the "equilibrium" outcome of the game is.

The direct interaction of the maximizer with the constraints she faces broadens the possibility for the emergence of "multiple equilibria". It sounds like a fancy term but in fact it is bad news for economists. The researcher has trouble knowing which of the multiple equilibria people will choose. Even more vexing is the possibility that people will settle into an equilibrium which is clearly worse for all. Ignorance is not the culprit. Everyone can see the prize. But in basic game theory they are unable to abandon their strategic maneuvering. Everybody may remain stuck in a sub Pareto-optimal state.

Public choice scholars may see support for their views in the bizarre, self-damaging equilibria that emerge from game theory. Significant adherents to public choice after all maintain that government and politics are inherently inefficient. If one views politics as a game between rival interest groups one could draw succor from the woes of game theory which has labored for decades to understand how its multiplicity of pathological equilibria could be remedied. The remedy proposed, known as mechanism design, also offers support to public choice scholars because it reserves for them an important role in saving political man from himself, something which Chicago dismisses as being unlikely.

Mechanism design

AFTER THE GREAT discoveries of the 1940's and 50's game theory grew arid. Interest revived in the 1970's when economists from the unrelated field of public finance started to investigate how lying and cheating degraded market efficiency. These problems plagued not only economics markets but politics as well.

Suppose government must decide between building a hospital or creating a national park, each of which will cost the same amount of money. How does it know which one to finance? Government could ask voters how much they are willing to pay, to see their preferred project go through above the per-person tax cost. The project for which people are willing to pay the most would be the one creating the most wealth in society. If all shared the cost equally then each voter would be tempted to overstate the value of her choice. By doing so she could skew the government decision towards her desired position without much of a concomitant increase in her personal cost. If the government is fooled into providing too much of the wrong project, then wealth is destroyed. The technical explanation is tedious but boils down to a situation in which a public good is provided to too many people at a cost which is above their valuation of it.

Game theorists saw in the problems of lying and cheating a useful extension of their science. By recognizing that strategic behavior in situations where some held more knowledge than others could be solved (that is, an equilibrium could be found) by using concepts from Bayesian statistics, game theorists were able to transform games of lying and cheating into games where everyone was honest and obedient. This, as you might quickly grasp, is no game at all. So in effect the theorists created a sort of "reverse game theory" in which government manipulated the rules and rewards of games to neuter all strategic comportment.

Here then was what seemed like a perfect opportunity for the social engineer to fashion clever game-theoretic suggestions on how to end lying and cheating in economics and politics. Such thinking suited public choice thinkers very nicely. The proliferation of sub Pareto-optimal equilibria that one discovered when examining relations between groups of people as game theoretic interactions gave public choice thinkers the chance to indulge their views that they had a prominent role to play in the salvation of politics. One often-cited example was provided by Nicolaus Tideman and Gordon Tullock in 1976.

Drawing on the work of previous researchers, Tideman and Tullock applied to politics the logic of something called a Vickrey-Clarke-Groves auction. It works by asking each person what the net benefit to him or her is above the per-person cost of providing the preferred alternative. You add up the dollar votes for the hospital and if the sum is greater than that for the park, the hospital gets built. But there is a catch. As well as getting charged the per-person cost of building the hospital, any voter who was "pivotal" in forcing the decision will pay an extra cost equal to the loss of net benefit to the other voters who did not see the park get created. "Pivotal" means that by announcing a high valuation on a certain outcome, it was you who tipped the political balance in its favour.

As Tideman and Tullock explained, "A nontruthful response cannot benefit the respondent, and it carries a risk of making him worse off than he would have been with the truth. If he understates his value, he may pass up an opportunity to obtain the result he desires at an attractive price. If he overstates his value, he may wind up paying more than it is worth to him to have his choice".

Correctly revealing your preferences is an equilibrium (of the sort named after Nobelist John Nash) because if everyone is expected to tell the truth, there is no profit for any single person to deviate from the truth. If we lie to get our way and others are telling the truth, we will be punished with an extra tax. If we lie by understating our preferences while others are honest, the compensation they pay will be proportional to our understated loss and thus not really enough to compensate us for our true loss of not seeing our preferred alternative go through.

Mechanism design's prescriptions for making politics efficient are so convoluted and difficult to understand that at present they have little hope of being found in the platforms of candidates running for office in the real world. We are perhaps closer to achieving the first human head transplant than we are to implementing anti-game theoretic rules in government.

Mechanism design however is a useful thought experiment on the manners in which we can become stuck in bad political equilibria. It also suggests how to escape these inferior states. Public choice makes similar claims yet the analogy with mechanism design is far from perfect. Both are built on completely different views of how decisions get made in society and how equilibrium is arrived at.

Conclusion

By now it should be clear that it is fruitless to judge whether Chicago or public choice have produced a better ultimate theory of power. Both share the same approach to understanding power. They apply utility maximization, monetary constraints, and equilibrium to behavior at the crossroads of politics and economics.

They differ in that Chicago political economy holds fast to the notion of political efficiency, whereas public choice heaps scorn on the concept. They differ also in their lines of attack. Public choice sees the world through the lens of the median voter model. It is freighted with assumptions, and this gives it precision. Chicago thinking is broad. It encompasses the median voter and many other possible models of political equilibrium. It applies to dictatorships as well as democracies. It dazzles researchers because it produces varied and nuanced predictions about government based on a few simple assumptions.

The parsimony of the Chicago approach to modeling politics finds many admirers within public choice, but provokes outrage and disbelief further afield. Chicago focuses on motives and not upon institutional structures. Such thinking is alien to political scientists. They are brought up to believe that institutions are important determinants of mass behavior. Chicago does not ignore institutions but rather considers them as endogenous. They emerge from more fundamental forces in the model. The endogenization of most aspects of human behavior is part of the broader Chicago method of reducing the explanatory variables of life to the barest minimum.

Despite the search for an ultimate theory of power led by Chicago and public choice, the word has not really gotten out yet to economists, let alone political scientists.

The message both schools try to transmit is that government policy cannot be analyzed outside of the context in which it is formulated. Pristine economic theories of cost-benefit analysis and optimal taxation have traditionally been formulated under the assumption that governments will carry out their prescriptions to the letter. Yet higher taxes, no matter how efficient they are will provoke tax evasion. More government spending on infrastructure will attract predatory interest groups who will lobby for preferential contracts. The plans of thinkers developed in an atmosphere of what Shackleton called "high theory" will come unravelled when imposed on competing interest groups.

Chicago judges the situation on two levels. At the lowest level we have rules of the political game that restrain interest groups. Within these rules such groups may seek to minimize the damage they do to the economy in order to minimize counter-reactions from other groups, but damage will nonetheless result from the antagonistic quest to seize resources from others. That is the narrow sense in which Chicago sees efficiency in politics evolving. However, it holds out more hope for the highest level of political action where the rules of the game are written. Becker and others believe constitutions with rules that limit rent-seeking may improve the tainted efficiency of the lower level political game. Public choice also believes in the importance of getting the rules right but feels that even the best rules will leave a political battlefield where notions of Pareto-efficiency are far from being realized.

It would be petty to denigrate one school or raise one above another. Despite their differences they both have done something no other thinkers have managed since the time of Plato. Chicago political economy and public choice are the first serious efforts to unite economics and politics into an equilibrium model, using consistent, mathematical logic. We are only beginning to appreciate what a revolution in thought their efforts have wrought. Yet the scarcity of published research on this revolution reminds one of the lengthy interval between Leeuwenhoek's observation of bacteria and Pasteur's discovery of a cure for rabies.

Further reading

Becker, Gary S. and Casey B. Mulligan (2003). "Deadweight Costs and the Size of Government." *Journal of Law and Economics*. 46:293-340.

Black, Duncan (1948). "On the Rationale of Group Decision-making." *Journal of Political Economy*. 56:23-34.

Brennan, Geoffrey and James M. Buchanan (1977). "Towards a Tax Constitution for Leviathan." *Journal of Public Economics*. 8:255-273.

Coase, Ronald H. (1974). "The Lighthouse in Economics." *The Journal of Law and Economics*. 17:357-376.

Downs, Anthony. *An Economic Theory of Democracy*. Harper. 1957.

Düppe, Till and E. Roy Weintraub. *Finding Equilibrium: Arrow, Debreu, McKenzie and the Problem of Scientific Credit*. Princeton University Press, 2014.

Harsanyi, John C. (1995). "Games with Incomplete Information." *American Economic Review*. 85: 291-303.

Hotelling, Harold (1929). "Stability in Competition." *The Economic Journal*. 39: 41-57.

McNeill, William H. *Plagues and Peoples*. Anchor. 1976.

Mueller, Dennis C. *Public Choice III*. Cambridge University Press. 2003.

Niskanen, William A. *Bureaucracy and Representative Government*. Aldine-Atherton 1971.

Olson, Mancur (1996). "Big Bills Left on the Sidewalk: Why Some Nations are Rich, and Others Poor." *The Journal of Economic Perspectives*. 10:3-24.

Rowley, Charles K. "Public Choice and Constitutional Political Economy". Pages 3-31 in *The Encyclopedia of Public Choice*. Edited by Charles Rowley and Friedrich Schneider. Springer. 2004.

Tideman, T. Nicolaus and Gordon Tullock (1976). "A New and Superior Process for Making Social Choices." *Journal of Political Economy*. 84: 1145-1159.

www.ingramcontent.com/pod-product-compliance
Lightning Source LLC
Chambersburg PA
CBHW032005190326
41520CB00007B/368